Looking Up!

Looking *Up!*

An Invitation to Compare Life Experience with Eternal Truth

Poems from the author of Crazy and Back!

James T. Edwards

XULON PRESS

Xulon Press
2301 Lucien Way #415
Maitland, FL 32751
407.339.4217
www.xulonpress.com

Paperback ISBN-13: 978-1-6628-3340-3
eBook ISBN-13: 978-1-6628-3341-0

Dedication

This book is dedicated to my father Herbert, who was there for me at the lowest point in my life.

I also would like to dedicate this book to my mother Leona whose hard-working servant spirit modeled a faithful wife and mother. I only regret I didn't appreciate her more during childhood.

My brother David should receive a dedication also. His outgoing, helpful spirit toward his high school peers gained me favor with others just because they knew I was his brother.

I dedicate this book finally to my wife Donna who endured my frustrating times in compiling this book and encouraged me to be patient.

I am grateful for all the input over the years from life's teachings, whether by teachers, writers, or revealed truths I would call, life's lessons. Practically, I want to thank my wife Donna for navigating the computer skills needed to complete my book.

Others I want to thank are Marc, Ken, Shari, and my many prayer-support friends.

Table of Contents

Introduction

This book of poetry is meant to be a follow-up to my first poetry book, *Crazy and Back*. My first book began with my journey as a teenager, not aware that God had any plan for my life. Not until the age of twenty-nine did I seriously decide to follow Jesus. By this book's title and subtitle, *Looking Up! An Invitation to Compare Life Experience with Eternal Truth*, I invite the reader to relate to me, and evaluate their own thoughts in life's journey.

Also, all those who read this book with an open spirit will confidently find that we can trust this loving Father, Savior, and Spirit of truth, who yearns to guide us in this life.

Chapter 1, *Poems about my Childhood and Youth Memories* should reveal common life experiences, some happy, some sad. In chapter 2, *Personal Testimonies*, "Same Difference" and "Connecting" exemplify the hopes and disappointments of social interactions. Chapter 3's *Poems of Prayerful Praise* attempt to show how authentic conversations with the heavenly Father will lead to praise and thanksgiving.

On a lighter entertainment side, in chapter 4, *Poems of TV and Movies*, you can see examples of a comedy sitcom in "Chosen Families" and of reality TV in "Traveling

Light." I suppose you could view the movie poems as recommendations and invitations to share fond memories of films I've liked.

One of my goals for this book is to encourage the reader to read the Bible for themself. Hopefully, chapter 5, *My Take on Bible Stories* will give you that desire. In "Authority's Glory," I portray a man of integrity and an attitude of honor that is so needed in our world today. "Extravagant Love" should evoke the desire to respond to God's love and see that Jesus Himself, as we should do also, took time out to receive love from those who love us.

Chapter 6, *Perspectives*—Some With, Some Without Scripture may be the most theologically controversial with "Widening the Narrow." Again, it's my take. I read the poem, "Forever," at an open mic night as a plea for each person to make the most important decision in this lifetime.

In Chapter 7, in *Family Plan*, I chose families old and new, with valued foundations. Families all need a unity of love. In chapter 8, *A Dream, a Vision, Visual Arts, Music, and Dance's* "Jazz Group" and "Fun Time," I experienced a free flow that came as I wrote them. In chapter 9, *Humor and Nonsense*, I arranged the poems from amusing real-life stories to nonsensical poetry. Which is which becomes obvious as you read them. Finally, in chapter 10, *Two Present-Age Parables;* both poems remind us of unrenewed thinking.

Chapter 1

Poems about Childhood and Youth Memories

Mother's Day Gift

It was mercy for me that day. Now it's too late to
honor you,
now that you left earth's stay. The honor I owe to you, I
can never repay.
My thankfulness I hope the Lord can relay.
Your servant heart made you so beautiful, although a
plain face;
your quiet appreciation was such strength.
My dad had, not too long ago extended our
modest house,
with a bedroom he laid out. With hard work and
afterwork hours
he deserved a rest in this family nest. Complete,
with bunk beds within, for my brother and me
to sleep in.
The first time I invited a new schoolmate over to play,
the challenge and appeal to best imitate the "man
of steel."
Leaping in a single bound from the bunk bed,
my playmate,
unlike me, rather to land in an upright stand, ended his
flight in the wall
with two holes, this stark reality staring at me. I'm told
the sheetrock of that day
was as cheap as its pay. Fear of my father entered my
center; thoughts of painful
punishment ended this anti-hero visit. I shot out looking
for my mother.
Coming from her part-time job, I spotted her
walking my way,

regarded by me as a divine appointment that jittery day.
She came at the exact time, a close-to-tears, fearful
son to find.
I begged her to not let my dad hurt me. Would she side
with Dad or with me?
There was no guarantee, though her gentle smile some-
what calmed me.
Hiding out 'til she had talked with my father first, I was
surprised and relieved.
My dad just warned me, never again, and dismissed me
with transferred grace.
On Mother's Day this year, I remembered my mom and
the protective gift she gave.

Silent Dad

Sometimes the truth, like rumors, can spread
like wildfire.
The body of this story resembles a skeleton; no answers
for why him?
Or, how come? A boy big enough to chase a dare,
playing with other boys, caught up in the frenzy
of activity,
could not from his zeal refrain, tried to hop a train.
Those in authority confirmed those questioning the story,
with a lead-in-line answering the mental picture, so gory.
The rescue crew could not save this boy, severed in two.
Much later, being a young boy myself, perhaps five
years younger,
I went into a neighborhood convenient store. What
for? As usual,
to buy some candy. When the clerk tallies the count,
handing me back the candy, he refuses to
take my money.
He simply nods his head, looking toward the back
by the bread. I quickly turn to see, the glimpse of a man
in greasy-looking mechanic's overalls, slightly smiling
at me before
he disappeared out the door.
The clerk, in a confidential, low voice, enough to hear
the drop of a pin,
tells me, he buys *all* the boy's candy when he's in.
I sense a tone of pain in his saying:
he's the man who lost his son to the train.

Uncle Avery

Thinking in later years, a memory returns so clear;
that of my mom's uncle Avery, a Pennsylvania
farmer, living
and working by himself outside in the manure-odor air,
fond of the comfort of beer. We would drive down to
visit a nearby aunt.
Oh, could she play her home piano, playing from hym-
nals, letting her worship fly, to
honor God Most High! Before we left, she'd mention
lonely Avery.
We'd basically stopped by to say hi!
In those days, cars had no AC, so we'd roll the windows
down to catch a breeze.
Coming from the field, Avery would greet us near his
home's property.
On his usual day, he'd be beer-breathed with
noticeable sway,
words slurred, leaning into the driver's open window.
We could smell him more than hear him. As a pre-teen I
always wondered
if he'd let us leave, for on one side of the front and
back windows,
he would wrap his arm around the post in between.
After about twenty minutes of sweet-tempered drunk-
enness he'd
became aware, his conversation to end. He bid us
a goodbye,
release his car-crutch, I think, for his bladder's need to
be relieved.

Many years later when I asked family about this over-
weight friendly man,
I was told, a corporate oil company discovered a
huge deposit
of oil on his land. They had lost touch since it sold. By
some we were told,
he left for Florida, his fortune to enjoy, the freezing win-
ters to avoid.
Due to his age, he must have already passed away;
I wondered,
could God have saved such as he? God, I know can
reach the desperate of soul.
Could his fortune have caused his death, or could it
have brought the provision
to show him the way to freedom, and God's power to
deliver him?

Kiss Discovery

I saw a movie about a young woman who wanted, for
her lips, a man
who would be ideal, for her first kiss. I reflected on this.
It took me back a bit to a life-changing event. It
seems I recall,
when in adolescence, I was with some mixed kids,
exchanging kisses,
you know, heterosexual explorations before puberty's
strong sensations. Anyway, for
my age, it seemed too close and physical, something I
really didn't much care about,
so I chickened out. Much later, during a summer break,
a friend of mine,
to meet with a girl, set up a time. I think she felt more
comfortable being
with a girlfriend, so for him to get close and appease the
girl's unease, as a favor,
I suppose, I came with him. I don't know who initiated
it, not me, just the same,
we wound up playing the "spin the bottle" game. It's a
game I'd never played
but knew of. After a long walk and a steep climb, I
appreciated this game, less active than
hide and seek. Of the two girls I could have spun the
bottle to, I had hoped it would point
to the smaller one, like me. I also judged her, the pret-
tier of the two. Wouldn't you know,
it stopped on the other. Being a late comer, never with
my lips, a girl had I kissed.

Standing to get closer, I realized, though of the same school year. this girl looked fully
mature. This girl, taller and more physically formed, had more to offer in excitability than
me. I held her lightly, as she bent down slightly. When our lips did engage, I realized this is something more powerful than a pretty face. It wasn't that her looks were a turn off, not at all, just not as pretty, a bigger frame and a little tall. But when our lips did fully meet, a whole new world opened to me. It was like fireworks going off explosively! I didn't want to disengage. She, after a short stay, pushed herself away. I sensed she had to end it that day, or someone needed to pour cold water on my body. Now, all I have
to say is, for me, it was something dangerous. Yet, I'll never forget, the power of a
mature female's kiss.

Chapter 2

Personal Testimonies

High Dive

Demeaned, seated naked with the other men, a small room held us NQSs—Non-Qualified Swimmers. Fellow Navy men mocked us with vigored whim—Why'd you join the Navy if you couldn't swim?

An instructor in a stoic, matter-of-fact way, instructed us how to swim on our backs that day. After a while, came the surprise.

In single file, we were ordered to climb the high dive. One of two decisions before us lay, jump or be pushed in unbalanced array.

Feeling shameful, each would have to float, our genitals to show. No time to be modest, seeking to hide from unmitigated pride. Around the pool a few marines stood, holding long poles wrapped with towels on the ends, to smack or to push each struggling man, 'til they swam or were allowed to grab the end, their lungs taking shaming water in. It was to sink in fear or test the water with the training you did hear.

Doubting myself more than my learning, as I jumped, inside my head I cried out, Jesus!

Hitting the water, I was flooded with a peace I'd never known. The Savior had come to my rescue. Clear as an audiotape playback I heard our instructor's words:

arch backward, head back, looking up, fill your lungs with air, hips even, pedal your feet like a bicycle, arms reaching back with overhead rotation scooping handfuls of water with each grasp. Seeing movement as I stared at the ceiling, I did glide straight to the other side.

Something more wonderful did happen inside. Right-on peace and joy came from the one whose name I called upon.

I spotted a struggling sailor clinging to the poolside coughing up water. With a newfound feeling of care, I asked, "Are you all right?" He nodded. A feeling of love for another person previously unknown had arose in me that day.

I hoped it would stay. Did Jesus baptize me that way? Years later, pursuing me, for His name's sake; a covenant commitment I did make.

Same Difference

When I reported to the Naval Communications Center
that day, I noticed a young black
man quietly observing me.
Later, he asked me about my fear. I denied it, though it
must have shown clear.
Two radiomen, though each a different race, would
become friends on Guantanamo base.
I suppose much was out of curiosity,
each coming from racially dominated communities:
black for him, white for me.
I wanted him to see my suburban/rural town
and he for me, his New York City home. So, we took
leave together.
First, we went to my proud past. I was naïve
and in shock.
All the friendly faces I knew from my youth turned stoic
toward us both.
Trying to hide regret and embarrassment, I suggested
we continue the trip.
To New York city we went. Similar, as his visit to
my hometown,
not a friendly face could be found. Faces froze, masking
emotions poorly,
unacceptance did show. Hey, a revelation to more
than some—
we aren't the defiant ones![1]
Though we lost touch, a few infrequent letters after our
time in the service,

---

[1] The Movie *Defiant Ones*, 1958.

the Cuba friendship held strong. I delighted to see the
pictures of his wife and family,
considering this man of character, a friend to me.

Evil Overcome

Working at the lab, as a young born-again man, though near thirty, I sought to show generosity. Though slim on money, I offered a co-worker with no transportation a ride whenever he needed one.

One night, headed out the door, I traveled a distance to a home church I'd been to before, its location I thought I knew. Forgetting, frustrated and confused, driving about, I couldn't find the right house.

A voice in my head said: If I was really serious about following Jesus, I'd have done my best and written down the address. For an excuse, my mind told me, you buried the place in your memory, the Lord is saying, "you really didn't want to serve Me!" Accusing myself, thinking, *I'm not worthy of the Divine, especially with a past like mine.*

Giving up the search after many failed attempts in the vicinity, I left for my apartment, as in a race. Feeling so unworthy, in such a hurry, I longed for my place.

There, standing on the curb near where I pulled in was my co-worker.

Hey Jim, could you give me a lift to a not-so-far bar? With a look of disgrace upon my face, I said: "Sorry man, I don't feel so good." Then the devil scored another hit: "You're just a lying hypocrite!" I, in a heap to deposit myself, literally fell to my knees in my closet. With desperate plea, I cried out for mercy! Jesus, forgive me! Peace flowed into my soul. I could see numbers before me:

They were chapters and verses. I quickly
grabbed my Bible.
Misery fled as the written words comforted me. I
inquired of another, the correct address.
At the next house church meeting, I spoke to a brother
before the teaching.
"Look what the Lord's been showing me." I read him the
three scriptures from my closet, I felt the Holy Spirit to
me, had shown, line upon line.
He responded in a bored tone, "Oh, that's what the
pastor taught on last time."

The Joy of Rejoicing

When I'm feeling down, I intentionally force myself
to abound.
It doesn't happen instantly; sacrificially, I sing songs
of praise.
I look to the permanent that will forever last, not the
temporary setback.
Emotions change when depression's gloom is defeated
by joy's tune.
The scripture states: "Because you did not serve the
Lord your God
with joyfulness, and gladness of heart, for the abun-
dance of all things, therefore you
shall serve your enemies." [2]

Yet, the Savior did step in, the only one without sin,
reversing the curse,
taking it upon him. So, let us rejoice in Love's choice
and receive Abraham's blessing. [3]
Abraham, father of faith, we will follow in the
pathway you trod,
becoming also friends of God. [4]
And like Paul and Silas, scourged and chained in jail,
without bail; [5]

---

[2] Deuteronomy 28:47a

[3] Galatians 3:13–14

[4] Romans 4:11; James 2:23

[5] Acts 16:23–25

let's sing praises to Christ our King, knowing freedom's
ring, not just for ourselves,
but for all who will hear Love's call. [6]

---

[6] Psalm 89:15–16

Immature Incident

When people speak of bad drivers, I refrain from
entering in the conversation.
When they might look for my view, I don't care to add a
thing or two.
For you see, at twenty-nine, as a baby Christian, I now
recall an incident of mine.
Driving a car one day, caught up singing praise, I failed
to see the red light
or the stopped car in front of me. Too late to hit the
brakes, the couple in the car in front
lunged forward, under attack from my car's impact. The
driver's head nodded a no, as in
his rearview mirror, he glared. Now aware of the angry
look on his face, to My Savior I
did pray for what to do, and what to say. Actually, for
myself the "h" word, I,
in my head, called out——HELP!
Upon seeing my smaller size, he seemed to inflate with
muscular pride.
Quickly getting out before he could reach me,
I expressed my apology for not paying attention.
In my mind,
I wanted to make compensation. As he looked over his
back bumper, a thought instantly
came to me; I asked him, *"How's your wife? Is she
all right?"* It seemed I
could see, conviction appear before me upon his face. I
realized what came to me to say
was God's grace that day. A tense moment did diffuse,
with not a moment to lose.

Upon bumper examination, he graciously spoke that
it appeared
there was no harm done.
Before he did leave, he pointedly warned me,
"In the future, pay attention."

Brotherhood Understood

It was a time in our lives, as young church brothers,
we pooled our meager resources to live with each other.
A group leader was assigned to keep some order.
Sometimes we'd try to condemn one
another with Bible verses, like wielding swords or jab-
bing with cutting words,
mainly to justify unexcused behavior. Though so dif-
ferent, we did try mostly to get
along. One had a guitar and would, in the evenings,
unite us in song.
One night, our leader, Mike, gave us something to do—
wash each other's feet.
Squirming with unease, we unenthusiastically agreed.
We set up a "hot chair," where,
I must confess, each brother would be richly blessed.
The one in the chair would sit, then all rotating clock-
wise, we would have a turn to be
prayed over, in the chair to receive the washing
of our feet,
and in a spirit of union, receive and serve communion.
The two on either side would serve him the bread and
the wine. An agreed prayer request
we did make. The brother standing behind the seat,
would receive from the Lord, and
give to the seated one, an encouraging Word.
Previously, at the start, we had asked the Lord to come.
Reverence and silence mingled
with the lessening of flesh.
Pride left the room, replaced by humility to share, both
to the one kneeling to wash the

feet and to the recipient in the chair. We prayed in the Spirit quietly,
'til feet were dry, and hearts self-examined during communion. Then to give a Word of
encouragement, it would take seeing each other by faith.
Hope would arise when we discovered Christ's love in us did abide.
Brotherhood was understood
when His will for another we did seek. Love would peak by choosing to be meek.

Co-Worker Friend

We became friends, another Christian guy and I. We
were co-workers
in two consecutive places, who, upon a lab closing,
along with two familiar faces,
were hired by another opening. Between the two loca-
tions, we'd spent over twenty years
of observations. He was from Georgia, me, New York
State. We'd reminisce about
western heroes, we'd seen on Saturday TV
shows as boys.
He is an African American, me, an American
Caucasian. One day,
to this friend I'd naively say, wasn't it great growing up
in that old-time day?
He replied with acumen: not so great where I
came from.
He never watched, to my knowledge movies or any
news event
about the '60s civil rights movement, I figured he didn't
want any thoughts to give,
to a mind-set he didn't want to relive. He'd gone
through high school class integrations
and played football on a team much like *Remember
the Titans.* [7]
Very competitive, but a team player and hard-working
man, he had helped me,
and I had helped him. Only recently had his youthful
environment hit me.

---

[7] *Remember the Titans*, Movie (2000), Directed by Boaz Yakin, screen-
play written by Gregory Allen Howard

It was on TV. It was about a man, struggling to
make a stand
in the movie, *Nothing but a Man.* [8]
It opened my eyes to the compromise of dignity, if they
were to love and provide for
their family, the African American endured. It's been
re-released. Hopefully it will
connect as a tool to remind us of the Bible's
Golden Rule. [9]

---

[8] *Nothing but a Man*, Movie (1963), Directed by Michael Roemer,
co-written by Roemer and Robert Young

[9] Luke 6:31"Do to others as you would like them to do to you" (NLT).

Liquid Love

I'd been dating a lady in years past, actually thirty-eight
as a matter-of-fact.
The relationship hit a snag for me. I desired a sprint for
a conclusion,
she, more of a marathon to depend on. I believed the
Lord did send her to me. By my
frequent calls to her, I sought myself content,
often called,
she wanted me only to relent. We had met in a prayer
group at church.
Even others said they could see a couple together we
should be,
though we sometimes doubted due to differing
personalities.
Friendship's camaraderie flowed steady.
Still, my pursuit stopped at a wall, impenetrable around
her heart.
For months regularly we met, yet without fuel, the fire
would go out.
She living at the beach and me about fifteen miles away,
we would seek to meet,
halfway for dinner and to talk.
One early eve to a restaurant we would go, both partial
to their steak, veggies, and yeast
roll. This night I hoped the fire of affection could
be stoked.
I believed that the Lord had given me the liberty to
pursue her as my wife.
But, because of her wall of self-protection,
I had some doubt that would ever work out.

We both had to work the next day. So, for a short stay,
we left, to our cars our goodbyes to say. In that parking
lot, behind the restaurant,
we'd once again, as numerous times before, hug
one another.
Upon our heads was poured, by the Spirit, a warm
liquid love,
sweet and thick like honey. That moment became sub-
lime, defining, transforming,
uniting, indelible in time. In that instance, the anointing
melted her wall of resistance. On
that occasion, so divine, that sign of God's persuasion
united us to give our
relationship time. A year after we met, we decided for
each other, we were the marrying kind.

A Work in Progress

Out of shape? Don't be bent. All you need do is repent.
We've all been wrong.
Swallow your pride. It's a lie.
What's to stumble when you fall into the arms of a
Savior so humble?
His tender care strengthens you above all you're to bear.
Sometimes no way out is the way out,
like people with slave-mentality pushed
back to the Red Sea; in their mind
killed or captured to serve their enemy.
Only by following God's awesome way
were they delivered that fateful day.
Potter, soften this misshapen clay.
With wetted hands, shape me within Your care,
fill me
and through me,
Your grace openly share.

Passion's Pride

While reading through an historical book, I came across a
fact that, to me
needed another look. [10]
In 1656, upon returning to his hometown, Boston, after
a voyage of three years at sea, Captain Kemble, on a
Sunday, greeted his wife with a kiss, "publicquely." In
breaking the religious spirit of the day, this passion
seeker would have to pay. Made to endure the blame,
with shame—his place for this public disgrace: two
hours, seated, with outstretched legs ankle-locked
in stocks.
I thought to myself, "He must have spent much
of that time meditating on, how, after all
this, another kiss could lead to such satis-
fying bliss." Did he try to hold back a grin
for this perceived public sin or just smile for
being a red-blooded American? Anyway, it
gave his wife plenty of time to prepare for
the tryst, pick up the house, and freshen up
a bit. He himself, may have needed to wash
his face from pharisaical thrown tomatoes,
eggs, or other vegs, he could not evade, seated
to behave. Perhaps, because it was a Sabbath
day, others too, could not enjoy the fun play,
of sporty pitching on a Sunday.
Still, the one who created man and woman's chemistry
told a more gracious story.

---

[10] *What Happened When, A Chronology of Life & Events in America*,
   p.41, Gorton Carruth, 1991

How should man construe, this special first weekday
true? He would simply say:
"The Sabbath was made for man, and not man made for
the Sabbath." [11]

Christ Characterized [12]

This poem is in honor of a man I knew. A pharmacist,
he left a position of very good earning to pursue a God-
given yearning
to help the poor. On a trip to Haiti he found in his heart,
it was hard to bear when children there had no
shoes to wear.
He sought to bring the "good news" by deed to
those in need,
reaching out to others who also would combine to bless,
from the US.
Remembering him, my wife would say, "Such a
nice man."
When he talked with you,
you felt so appreciated.
His warm and welcoming grin drew you in.
His rich drawl spoke southern gentleman. Later, to
remote villages,
to city and nations, he believed God sent him, he
would come
to declare God's kingdom! He spoke boldly and cried
out inside
for God to prove Himself, whom he had bragged about.
When he gave an invitation to come down, God would
show up strong,
with miracles that would astound.
Through Ed's ministry, thirty-two churches were
birthed in Haiti.

---

[12] Caribbean Ministries International, Ed H. Floyd Jr., Director
(deceased)

A humble man, in the sense, he believed in the greater
works Jesus promised.
His wife would join him in prayer and counseling. Both
bold and hopeful
with God on their side, they went forward together in
confident stride.
At their commands, in Jesus's name demons would flee.
He passed away
after a life of faith to obey. Five confirmed dead,
through their ministry were raised.

Overlooked [13]

Now that I'm retired, my eyes seem to ferret out the
once-disguised.
The job and fitting needs into a schedule had blinded
me, not to see
the thousands of things I'd overlooked, that time failed
to book, even sparingly.
I'm not OCD, for litter and dust had crept up on me. I'd
find oversight on my part,
but becoming aware in tiredness, I'd acquiesce
permissively.
Now, always something—the dogs' water bowl is empty.
The fridge, filtered-water pitcher goes to a whole new
level low.
There's a corollary between caring for my house, while
caring for my body.
I contemplate why a hedge trimmed levelly can so
quickly grow unevenly.
When I worked for a living, Friday's
eat-out-with-wife-night
found us hurrying to relax. Yet, the sight of
happy couples,
families laughing and enjoying each's company, was
my delight.
Planners with time blocks, to quell the overdue,
each procrastinating task, glaring for attention, never
seeming to lack.
Age has slowed me down, 'til I've found time to enjoy
the overlooked pleasures

---

[13] This poem does not negate, in any way, my reaching out with the
good news to those Jesus would call me to.

as well. I'm reminded again to do all things as unto Him. Feelings can come and go. I'll practice His presence. Enjoy Him loving me. Letting myself accept more of His grace.

I'll give thanks in everything. And, I'll insist there's no need to catch up

when I set my pace and enjoy my place.

Connecting

Age and beauty become one
when her eyes sparkle in a brief twinkle of connecting,
a point made, a point well-taken. It's an affirmation of
appreciation.
No, I'm not fishing for a compliment, just expressing an
opinion that I could relent,
if she presented a viable alternative argument.
Soul surfing, I suppose you could call it.
Where will this friendly flow of connecting go?
Will it lead to a higher elevation,
a promotion of character, hope?
Will love from above bless this parlance?
Exchanging our cutlery and files,
sharpening our views, dissecting truths,
our hearts esteemed, we become quite a team.[14]

---

[14] Proverbs 27:17 (NLT)

Unknown Rifts

Just an observer, the story's a mystery to me.
At a drive-by glance, I viewed what seemed a thir-
ty-something couple on a
corner, she, much smaller, being held tightly,
crying and shaking in his embrace. He holds her physi-
cally in place.
I see a need for God's grace. My mind questions whether
this relationship will
change to an emotionally secure one, or, a love-hate one,
continuing to reoccur.
Giving it to the Lord, I pray. Only He can reach
them anyway.
To correct and combine with His love and respect, or
separate the two,
not to look at each other, but at Him, the perfect Lover.
Another two, I've talked to each separately. They're ten-
ants that conflict,
living in the same apartment complex. Next-floor
neighbors,
he calling her "the devil-woman" downstairs,
she, complaining of his family's noisiness, and
breaking the rules
of the building's shared space. I listened uncomfortably
as each accused the other to me privately.
I made a pact with my tongue not to take a side, not to
reveal to each,
the other's mention, refusing to judge gossip's deception.
I pray, dear God, only You know the truth. For, at times,
I feel the need for help, to remove the beam from my
own eye. I pray,

Father today show them the Lord's forgiving way.
In my fantasy I see, to avoid those offended,
coming before judgment courts; could we do a plea bar-
gaining of sorts?
Each party signs a form, agreeing to judge themselves,
saving the judge's time. With this mutual agreement,
acted in good faith, each will release one another,
reconciled by peace and grace.

The Elastic Mile

From a childhood in a small suburban town, then traveling and relocating,
upon returning from a long time gone, I was amazed at how much smaller
seemed the former space. The mile walk I would sometimes, in my youth take,
which now that I think of, seems to shrink.
The proximity of each building,
now seems to consume the in-between. It is as if the structures;
miniaturized illusions—the town inhabited by Lilliputians. [15]
Had my universe expanded? Time and travel altered my comprehension.
Perhaps experiencing big city blocks and huge buildings stretched
my mind's perception. Is the extra mile Jesus told us to go,
relative to our now, when our minds need to grow?[16]
Perhaps there's an elasticity
that comes with maturity. An aging and a shortened stride for me, presently
makes for energy's sacrifice, when the decision to pamper my body
or helping another does collide.
I recently felt my leg being "pulled" by the King I am to behold.

---

[15] Reference from *Gulliver's Travels*, Jonathan Swift, 1726.

[16] Matthew 5:41

I had just heated up a late supper. Before to fork the first
mouthful, my cell phone rang,
for me, a sound sorrowful. After a brief, ignored delay, I
called the widow back.
Chronic pain and anxiety,
a desperate need, caused her to seek a praying
friend to agree
for her good Lord's relief. I easily complied,
with her yeses and amens,
to which my words of faith did
coincide. The next day, as a pre-evening nap I had pres-
ently sought, she called me back.

Once again, the ring I sought to ignore. Then, I thought
it might be important.
I couldn't pretend that I was not present on the other
end. Immediately
upon returning her call, I was very encouraged,
as she unloaded a thankful testimony on me.
She did say, she had awakened the next day,
feeling so much better because for her I did pray.
Our Father's comforting grace had taken place.
There's no extra mile in God's time and space.
Yet, for me to grow in grace,
a stretch of mental distance must take place;
a distance for me I must be prepared to breach.

Retirement?

Thank You Lord for retirement.
Now I don't have to clutter up my life with employer's strife,
always seeking to one-up on the competition.
Thank you that my health did hold up, my expenditures mostly to bear,
for social security's still there, along with Your return blessings that flow.
Show me what to give and where to sow, like a stent for my spirit's heart-flow.
So many good works to give to; I pray o'er the cards in my hand,
Lord, should I up the ante? Hold or fold?
Now under Your freedom's management, I can volunteer for
or support Your start-ups. Also, established missions, I love to see,
long faces becoming thankful smiles, families strengthened by Thee.
Upon Your return, reward-giving Father, I'll be praying,
doing my part of Your plans, extending that promised blessing,
from Your benevolent hand!

Pulling Weeds While Aging

Perhaps it's just a personal quirk, but an undesired look
calls me to work.
I call the project my brick garden. It's not a
brick walkway,
nor do I grow vegetables or flowers. A previous owner
left a four-brick
wide, side by side, twenty-four-foot-long bricked
enclosure,
lined with cut cinder blocks, standing up.
It's a framed work of art to me, unless between the
bricks or border there
are weeds to see.
This unique look also gives the meter reader a firm
place to stand,
when he reads our meter by hand. Though, nothing but
natural dirt between
the bricks does hold,
lined with cinder-block parts to provide a firm mold.
The undesired look comes when I let weeds grow,
neglecting a clean look to show.
I choose parts of the day that provide the most shade.
With my hand-held bucket, I search each weed
to pluck it.
My system also reminds me of my plan to view
life. I work,
looking back to see the progress I've made,
not turning my head forward abrupt, judging
what's ahead,
tempted to give up. The pile of weeds in the bucket
makes progress seem

stronger. I think to myself, "It can't be much longer."
Bending down,
while on the bordered cut cinder blocks, pulling
the weeds,
I start to see, the traditional, look of red clay,
still likeable for this present day.
When I finally reach the end,
I would have perhaps stopped, or quit,
rejecting neatness's lure, if I considered my legs'
stiffness,
and chose not to endure.
Perhaps pushing myself, knowing more weeds will
grow again
(I like environmental naturalism, protecting
nature and man),
I feel better about myself and believe the effort will spill
over some,
to persevere when other challenges come.
A handyman might wonder, why not, for the better, pull
the bricks up, and
cement them together.
Over time that would be fine, yet, my age being old,
I'm more looking forward to walking on a street
of gold. [17]

---

[17] Revelation 21:21

Same Page for Today

My pastor assigned us to read of the birth and
life of Jesus.
Beginning in December, in Luke each day, we were to
read a chapter.
Then after, finishing on Christmas eve, the twenty-fourth,
we'd be cognizant of the wondrous meaning of the life
of this Servant King.
God Himself would display a spectacular heavenly
sight so bright
to the poor, bottom-rung-of-the ladder shepherds,
that angelic night! On the twenty-fifth of this December
we collectively knew, having read Luke,
what this God-Child did do.
At home we could see the greatest present wasn't
under a tree.
For He came into a cold, broken world with issues
that like ours now still needs The Good News.
Though at the stable where "the fair baby lay" it may
have been a "Silent Night," [18]
it can be said, that God's garden pledge, [19]
by this newborn's life, would herald "Love in
any Language"
and would be "fluently spoken here."

---

[18] The hymn, "Silent Night, Holy Night" Words: Joseph Mohr 1818,
Music: Franz Gruber 1818.

[19] Genesis 3:15b.
The song, "Love in any Language" Written by John Mohr and John
Mays for Sandi Patty 1986

Christmas—Easter

Walking my neighborhood, I took in colorful lights of
good cheer.
It's that celebratory time of year!
For as God gave His Son, that spirit of giving
touches everyone.
But for some, lost loved ones, leave memories lonely
and distant.
For others, broken relationships over staunch
disagreements
built walls of impenetrable resistance. Though, for
most kids,
the festive lights and holiday hopes lifts their spirits
for parental and family blessings. Even Hanukah,
with its natural candlelight makes aglow, smiling faces.
On the second street over from mine, I'm aston-
ished to find,
a scene I thought at first, incomplete. It seemed the
main point missing,
leaving a manger trough filled with hay. Did someone
steal the baby?
No other figures there, this scene so bare. No lights,
even for nights,
the world's light had gone.
I felt like Mary at the tomb, looking for missing Jesus.
He also had journeyed far from the womb,
from birth's crib, His life to completely give.
Perhaps the owners were making a Christmas–Easter
type decree.
This babe, Immanuel, left heaven's glory for you and me.
The shepherds sought Him out that day.

Now, we can become one with Him,
dead to sin and alive in Him, raised by His resurrection.[20]

---

[20] Romans 6:5

Chapter 3

Poems of Prayerful Praise

Harp and Bowl

How do I stay focused when I commune with God?
Alone, I can implement
the revelation with a heavenly look from the Bible's
last book.
Prayer's flow can be continued when we follow this
principle—harp and bowl. [21]
It's never fickle to follow the IHOP version led by
Mike Bickle. [22]
Founded on heaven's model in the Bible, it is to alter-
nate music (the harp)
with prayers (the bowl) to engage with the Lord.
We bring songs of thankfulness, honoring Him in praise
and worship,
the fruit of our lips.[23] Then we pray His will, aligning
our requests to His promises.[24]
It kind of reminds me of those school tests we took,
when all the teacher did look for were answers found in
the study book.
Yet, we are not graded. We lose ourselves when He
is elevated.
Each song brings to mind our requests with thankful-
ness: fresh faith,
birthing hope's strength. Sometimes a God-sent Word
comes through a person who heard, not knowing the
circumstance to which it referred,

---

[21] Revelation 5:8

[22] Mike Bickle, director of the International House of Prayer, Kansas City, Missouri.

[23] Hebrews 13:15

[24] 1 John 5:14–15

revealing, God is always aware, and wants to show His personal care.

Pauses are made to give praise testimonies for past prayers answered.

Uplifting words edify all who come, oppositions become undone,

reminding us that His victorious promises we can stand upon.

High Praises

I asked myself, how do the high praises of God arise? [25]
Don't they come from deep inside, when we realize
how awesome is our sovereign God? I've had
times when
I clearly saw a breakthrough, an answer to my prayer;
hope renewed!
Responding to His faithfulness, I shouted true.
Immediately I knew,
to sustain this praise, I'd need a body from heaven's
source, one glorified, of course,
for my throat not to go hoarse. A praise I would give, so
much better,
more enduring to heaven's king, like the line in the
Vineyard music song:
"I could Sing of Your Love Forever!" [26]
My thoughts leaped to heaven. Gathered before the
throne the
voices of the saints arise, 'til they can be heard, along
with the angels.[27] On earth, as
high praises of God in our mouths exalt the
most-high God,
the Spirit of Truth makes us free, binding the enemy,
from our life's entry. [28]
As corporate worship in unity commands God's blessing,
He inhabits our praises,

---

[25] Psalm 149:6

[26] LIFESCAPES, praise and worship, grateful joyous praise, 2001 compass productions.

[27] Psalm 148:2

[28] John 8:32, Psalm 149:6, 8

bringing us into His presence, surrounding us with songs of deliverance. [29]

We are aware. We are truly before Your throne, so pure. Then, holiness and silence pervade the atmosphere, and all in unison we await to hear, the voice of the one most dear. [30]

---

[29] Psalm 133:3b; 22:3; 32:7 (NKJV).

[30] Revelation 8:1 (NKJV).

Response, a Prayer Poem

I thank you, Lord, for the hope that lives within You. I thank you, Lord,
for Your Spirit so true. I thank you, Lord, God of the angels, for it's You
who enables the weak to be strong. Those looking down, forlorn,
can find acceptance by You and be reborn.
Restore our souls, lighten our loads, and define our minds by Your spoken words' flow,
washing away past harmful imbedded words' decay.
Oh, God, our Maker, how grand and important we appear in Your hand. Savior,
like a precious, indelible, constant memory offered in humility,
You became our prize, our victory! May I always seek to please.
Keep my mind in Your peace, abiding and growing in You, never amiss,
each answer from a clear conscience; right with You,
for You are here now, right here with me.
The words: I love You seem empty. Give me help to obey each opportunity,
to love, to equate, my thankful heart, with my eyes upon You, moving,
demonstrating love's cost, while carrying my cross.
By following You, I appreciate the something
You've made me to be, for without You, I am nothing.

Wandering Thinking

Now that I'm Yours, I know I've already been forgiven.
Still, I'm trying to realize
just how You see me through a redeeming Father's eyes.
Is it humorous to You when my lips keep going, while
my mind wanders off
to unrelated thoughts? If you were a human dad
standing here,
wouldn't your child seem strangely queer,
forgetting in mid-sentence what he was saying? He had
left eye contact,
enticed by mind's flow; now looking out the window.
What if this child of Yours,
sir, had just asked you in earnest, you did assume,
a question, and before you could reply, hurriedly
left the room?
Considering Father God, did familiarity distance me
from focused reverence?
I know true, there's no condemnation toward me from
You. Did You, who knew all
things with omniscient perspective,
from beginning to end, know that grace, in matu-
rity's pace,
would these wandering thoughts replace?
Holy Spirit Guide, straighten my head from turning
side to side.
Help me to see You looking at me, as a good Father,
delighting to please.
Turn up my spirit's hearing to drown out each dis-
tracting sound.
Give me super-quick ability to immediately cast down

all thoughts that keep our conversation from
flowing free!

Real Places in the Heart

If we truly care for someone, won't we spend time in
prayer for them?
In prayer, we sense God's hope and call for each and all.
Look at the reaction of Samuel at the removal of Saul as
Israel's king—
God had to call him out of mourning.[31] Previously, at
Saul's coronation,
Samuel presented the man to all and vowed not to sin
by failing to pray for him and them. [32]
How could Apostle Paul thank the heavenly Father for
the Philippian Christians? [33] Though apart, in a letter
he'd confess,
he had them in his heart.[34] Finally, I think you'd
agree, Epaphras
was a man who carried faces and places in his heart.
His fervent prayers kept open his heart's door,
laboring by travels for those he cared for.
One more thing I would add: before I became a follower
of Christ,
a friend in the Navy made several attempts to bring me
to eternal life.
I refused, even finding myself slightly amused,
when this man cried because he cared. I never forgot
those tears

---

[31]   1 Samuel 16:1a

[32]   1 Samuel 12:23

[33]   Philippians 1:3

[34]   Philippians 1:7

that told me true, in his heart, I had found a place.
In heaven I'll thank him face to face. [35] [36]

---

[35] Colossians 1:7; 4:12–13

[36] The sailor's name was Charles Pierce.

Interrogatives' Lure

Though disobedience caused mankind to eat from the
wrong tree,
another human trait could have contributed to that fate,
when the forbidden fruit they ate—curiosity.
I read some info from the leader of a ministry. [37]
He mentioned, so positive, about how he prayed, using
interrogatives.
Satan spoke to the two, accusing God of telling
them a lie
("Surely you shall not die"). Adam and Eve saw
the fruit that looked so good to eat and probably
wondered why.
Why, out of curiosity. Like all the other fruit, it looked
like a sweet treat.[38]
So, to pray effectively for another person, it makes sense
to appeal to the intrinsic query
in them. The prayer leader, in his monthly pamphlet,
advised to pray
with assurance and fervency for the Holy Spirit to plant
questions in them,
then, lead them, to "The Truth," the "Who," God sent for
me and you.
For instance, why? Why am I alive? Or what? What am
I here for?
How? How can I know? When? When will I be free from
pain and suffering?

---

[37] Dick Eastman, Every Home for Christ Ministry, 640 Chapel Hills
Drive, Colorado Springs, Co. 80920 USA.

[38] Based on Genesis 3:4–6

Which? Which course should I take? Who? Who has the
answers for me?
Where? Where can I go to find peace and contentment?
Then we can pray: Father God,
give them the answer: the gospel of Jesus, witnessed by
an authentic believer.
Upon further reflection, my thoughts of curiosity travel
an opposite direction.
Seeing that you and I inherited a fallen nature through
original sin;
perhaps that's where curiosity did begin. Or, maybe, it
was an innate trait designed for
man in God's original plan, before the fall to help us
seek answers from Him. I believe
it was really Satan's deception, not curiosity, that caused
Adam and Eve, and thus, all of
us, to return to dust.

Incognito's Other Side

What causes Clark Kent to spring into action? Isn't it the affront
to justice, truth, and the American way? Here's an idea
that's come in its time: fictional characters like Wonder Woman,
Black Panther, Batman and Robin and so many others; don't
they respond to life-and-death needs of humanity's sisters and brothers?
What if a hard-hearted man or woman received salvation,
placing the Supreme's superpower in them,
their hearts transformed to call for God's grace
in prayer? [39]
Weak in the knees, bent by fears, one finds peace with the casting of
cares.[40] For, with heaven's flow comes great and mighty things,
strong exploits to show things one did not know.[41]
What if motives could be pure, obeying the truth He's assigned you to do?
What if, with love's currency we could spend freely? Not all who could
use a personal gift receive it willingly.
Tell them that some things for you were hard to receive too. It took humility.

---

[39]   Hebrews 4:16

[40]   I Peter 5:6

[41]   Jeremiah 33:3

To receive the gift, you might say, took an attitude shift.
Thankfulness held sway that day, for pride in me, not
to abide.[42]
Yet, praying for them first could very well pave the way,
even what to, or
what not to say.

---

[42] I Peter 5:5

Make us like:

Dear God, make us like pie crust, ready to fit in your baking dish.
Fill us to the taste You want to present. Lemon, chocolate, fruity fillings,
both for warming or serving cold, so thrilling. When they taste our offering,
they would know they tasted of You, soooo good! Make us refreshing,
cold and thirst-quenching, like a fountain, with Life springing.
Also, make us salty, with the reality of victories won,
by hard times lived through, having put our trust in You.
May the source of this fountain draw them to hydrate,
and revitalized by Your living water to saturate.
Make us like God's travel agents, helping to bridge connections
for each's journey in Your company. Make us like an all-purpose rachet set.
Use us, by Your Spirit, to loosen or tighten emotions amiss.
Make us negotiators of peace, diffusing possible catastrophes.
Yes, and for gaps in tranquility, Prince of Peace,
make us like You: repairers of the breach.
Make us like innocent playmates of children, bringing fun.
Build memories for them, mind-sets so wholesome.
Make us like tubes to squeeze,
holding pastes to please, for helpful needs. Make us like toothpaste to clean,

calk to seal, glue to adhere, aloe to heal.
Make us like spiritual make-over artists, bringing beauty's overflow,
satisfying one's self, with radiant glow. Heavenly Father, we thank
you for all the blessings You've given for man to discover.
But mostly, we thank you for being so faithful and true.
We'll find You, we'll suit, being branches of the Vine, bearing fruit.[43]
For every good and perfect gift is from You.[44]

---

[43] John 15:5

[44] James 1:17

Either/Or

Many each day know physical pain and suffering. In
various ways,
the hurting seek relief. Then, there are congenital inher-
ited defects,
needing remedies not to neglect. Others wait in hope,
having an illness terminal,
for a scientific cure. Twisted limbs, club feet, cleft pal-
ates, degenerative disorders,
unresolved by doctors' orders. Others pay for expensive
medical care that only sustains
life, not to repair. How did the Perfect Healer and
Miracle-Worker,
while on earth as God's and man's son, face
this problem?
There was only two ways Jesus healed: either He
went to them,
or, they came to Him.[45] You might say, what about when
He spoke healing,
when the recipient was away? Yes, like the centurion's
servant, and the
Syrophoenician woman's daughter; each request was
made by proxy.[46]
Like our prayers to healing's source, as in heaven, Jesus
brought healing to earth. [47]
If Jesus gave healing by proxy, by a loved one standing
in, we also can benevolently

---

[45] Mark 6:6 (NKJV); 54–56

[46] Matthew 8:13 (NKJV); Mark 7:29–30

[47] Luke 11:1–2.

carry their request to Him. You may say, may I pray for
you in Jesus's name? Didn't He
ask an individual, "What do you want me to do for you?
[48] Wouldn't the one who
healed, everyone to Him who'd come, accept our
request and reveal His love by His
power to heal?

---

[48] Luke 18:40.

One

He greeted hello, but my voice did flow.
His love broke through, but it was I who
smiled at you.
That door I opened for you,
it was His right hand, His honor to you imbue.
And, when you said, "Thanks,"
though I heard it, I echoed it to Him too.
I could see your hands were full when I opened
that door.
As long as your head isn't full of you,
there's room for honest exchanges of truth,
a conversation inviting your participation.
To me, the extra mile would take my listening ear.
I silently pray, Lord, help me, attention to pay,
to relate Your heart-to-heart, please translate.
Let me introduce You to him.
Show me where to begin.

Beyond Me

I praise and thank You for giving me assign-
ments I can do,
for I can do all things through You.
Whether a quick work or a lifetime to achieve,
with You, no feat will I not complete.
Though parts lay strewn from time to time,
You give the wisdom to assemble as one—
a good work, leaving nothing undone.
In answer to prayer, surprisingly, another guided by Your
shepherd care,
helps assist me where I lack.
The joy You give comes with expectant hope;
for what You've done before, You can do again, yielding
so much more.
If I eye the task with present strength to draw upon,
I'll fall short without Your Name to call on.
But tapping into the extra-mile strength of You in me,
I'll experience victorious joy, in united harmony.

Chapter 4

Poems of TV and Movies

Back to Our Future

Back in the fifties, the TV show, *You Are There*, attempted to make
historical events clear, with the premise you can go back to any day and year.
America's most trusted anchor of nightly news, Walter Cronkite, questioning
famous people, did the interviews. These encounters of interest brought time
alive. More than dates for tests to memorize, through the interviews we
understood people shaped by and shaping their times. I thought to myself,
What if past great Bible teachers and preachers could time-travel to hear Jesus's expository message preached to two, that resurrection year?
Jesus joining them made a threesome: Cleopas and the unidentified one, (now
vicariously, all believers, viewing from heaven). Along that road to Emmaus,
Messiah, restraining their eyes, came alongside. He asked what they were
discussing. Their reply inferred,
Where have you been?
Hadn't he heard the recent news from Jerusalem? They expressed their hope, now gone, for they had
hoped for the Messiah-King to set up His kingdom. Unraveling the mystery in their minds, He
expounded on scriptures from Moses

through all the prophets. Wouldn't this be, from the one who taught with
authority, the greatest sermon from, the one who lived *The Greatest Story Ever Told?* [49]

I thought again about those powerful preachers and teachers, listening and seeing the King, for them nothing could be as exciting! George Whitfield, John Wesley, Charles Spurgeon, Billy Graham, Reinhard Bonnke and others also experienced their hearts burn within them as they heard, from the Word Made Flesh" the Rhema Word.

Perhaps to help us 'til heaven's place, to bridge the space, we can listen to the video on YouTube: "That's My King," preached by J. M. Lockridge.

---

[49] From Luke 24:13–27

Chosen TV Families

It's the desire of many to choose a TV family. We
choose one
we'd like for kin or an extended group we'd like to fit in.
For example, as a boy I liked to see, *My Three
Sons*. I would
have liked a dad as wise and generous as
Steven Douglas.
For a family well-known and respected in the
community,
one might befriend Andy, Opie, and Aunt Bee
of Mayberry.
If you're an urbanite and have a strong yearning to
thrive, despite all the jive,
you can relate to J. J. in *Good Times*. He's dynomite!
I always enjoyed the glib humor of *Alf*, the alien from
planet Melmac
taken in by a loving family, yet always wanting to eat
their cat.
A large family whose family values always astounds me;
The Waltons. Oh, such
family unity! It's evident when each endeared resident is
waited for together by this
family, upon a return home, or leaving a while from
such harmony.
Did you ever want to be part of a diversified group?
There's plenty of jesting and bantering wit, with
Hawkeye in the army's *MASH* unit.
How about a son who honors his pop,
though his dad's plans delightfully flop?
It's the twosome of *Sanford and Son*.

How about a wife and mother who won't relent,
but defends her good sense
on *Home Improvement*? Though Tim's the handyman,
with the boys Jill often has the upper hand.
You can spend some comforting couch-potato time for a
while and vegetate,
as you enjoy happily, your chosen TV family.

Traveling Light

Faith's adventure begins totally dependent on Him. Can we learn from
those less fortunate, having skills we do not? For example, it's not a loss
to think of the TV show, *Undercover Boss*. To investigate bottlenecks,
inconsistencies, production/service, and labor costs, this is the job for "incognito
boss." He or she sheds the superhero suit, disguising themselves to get to the
truth. Venturing out to their employees' camp, seeking to discover what to
revamp. With a brave or presumptuous foot forward, they, through prearranged
reciprocal ploys, convince managers to train them as candidates for their own
franchise start-ups, or possible applicants to employ. Either way: to evaluate, and
to or not to recommend. You may think these under-cover CEOs are taking
uncomfortable, exposed, vulnerable positions, just for name brand recognition,
a disingenuous notion for product promotion. Yet unforeseen days, while
working together, yield heartfelt ways. With a listening ear, they hear
the personal family struggle of certain employees with empathetic concern.
A few who had bad attitudes, upon employer's inspec-tion, would later be subject

to authority's correction. Those loyal servants who envision the business as a

career, will, with the CEO, find a listening ear. Even those whose passions lie

elsewhere will oft discover a benevolent friend to help alleviate burdens, opening

doors, their spirits to soar. At the end comes the reveal, the ridiculous disguise

comes off. To each employed may come thoughts: my complaints or my

frankness just cost me my job. Yet these workers' values are rewarded with

additional training for supervisory position and higher pay. Also, often comes

help for their family from the exec, who once worked hard to overcome life

struggles 'til affirming personal vision's respect. Yet thoughts did come

to the higher-ups, stripping themselves of all the home stuff, stepping out,

relinquishing their clout; remembering back to when all they had was a dream.

Now they want to feed the dreams of others by meeting their heart-long needs.

Antiques Roadshow Imagination

Watching an episode of *The Antiques Roadshow,*
those who know,
the rarity, originality, and what each craftsman's done,
appraise each item.
Other factors can enter in. Did it reflect its peri-
od's history?
Was the generational heirloom documented to notable
biography?
The older the better, and rival factions fighting to claim
each attraction
can add to auction's sum.
How valuable if a one-of-a-kind was combined to price-
less history?
What if an antique was never lost but handed down the
family line,
verified by scientific testing in present time?
I'm referring to a seamless robe from the greatest story
ever told. What if this
was the actual garment Christ did wear, that day our
sins to bear?
And what if in that special unit, the winning soldier
casting the lot for that tunic
was the same, who at the Savior's death, declared out
loud, truly this man who
died was the Son of God! And what if a scroll accompa-
nied this gift to his family,
and this artifact gave testimony, describing three hours
of darkness that day,
before heaven's King for us the price did pay?

This centurion could have written of this Man, scorned and mocked,
preparing for care His mother, assuring salvation's belief to a dying thief,
forgiving in shame those who disgraced His name. And even committing His
spirit to His Father in faith, honoring all men, faithful to the end. You say, that
was way long, long, long ago, no way. But I say, if this Roman soldier was
destined to win the curious cloth from his peers, could not the one who blessed
him keep it, to reveal it after two millennial years? For this priceless treasure,
what cost could one measure? What if his family line were secretive, treating it as
a household shrine? Time will most likely never affirm my holy imagination. Yet,
for this guy, I'm looking up, 'til Jesus splits the sky.

Two Displays

I saw a *Stories from the Stage* on PBS. Although multiple truths were conveyed,
one for me had much to say. The woman spoke with endearment about her
Iranian uncle's first-time American visit. He loved this land of opportunity.
He asked to see Ellis Island and the Statue of Liberty.
In the tour boat on the way, she told of their delight viewing New York's skyline sight.
She found it a challenge to include her uncle and her in a selfie with a background of
Lady Liberty. While she accommodated him, they conversed in Farsi.
Inquiring several times in soft tones, she spoke to a couple sitting in front of them.
When no response came, she tapped the man on his shoulder lightly,
asking nicely, "Would you take a picture of my uncle and me?"
Plainly irritated, before he could bring a word, his wife through her clenched teeth did blurt, "Don't give them anything!"
Hurt beyond words, this previously proud-to-be-an-American tried to hide her tears.
Her uncle, in Middle Eastern tongue comforted true, "Dear, don't let it bother you."
After, when another couple saw her struggling to take their picture,
offered to, then taking it with amiable pleasure. Of course, you might surmise,

each country has citizens that show hate and love,
yet that day,
I saw two kingdoms, one of intolerance to display,
another of acceptance, a higher citizenship to obey.

A Few Movie Memories

As an idealistic youth, *Spartacus* to me rang true. My favorite scene
was when I heard freedom ring; each warrior brother would cry out, "I'm Spartacus!"
in covenant unity. Later, in history, Patrick Henry would agree with the rest,
and loudly protest, "Give me liberty or give me death!"
All at once, Lucy, the character played by Sandra Bullock in
While You Were Sleeping, was surrounded by family acceptance.
It seemed pleasantly overwhelming to me. Her deception,
yet her need to be loved, lead to such a warm family reception.
She eventually became part of that well-cast family, finding the more compatible
brother, to marry.
An all-time favorite for me, I wished they'd have it more on TV: *A Tree Grows in*
Brooklyn. It's so good for the eyes when you need a good cry,
yet usually my throat gets too choked. The story shows a flawed father,
yet how a kind-hearted, and a kingly-type blessing he could be.
Touching his daughter's heart even after his death, breaking through her dearth,
revealing the title analogy: the severed tree, growing back up through cemented earth.

If ever a situation called for righteous indignation, it
came in a scene, we can
one hundred percent agree. *In Back to the Future,* cow-
ardly George
found life-saving redemption and meted out jus-
tice to Biff,
bringing his aggression to a halt, rendering a
powerful hit,
rescuing Lorraine from sexual assault.
We see, how being liberated from fear can change our
whole future.
The '98 movie, *Les Misérables,* revealed how a life
transformed by an act of grace could lead to such
good place.
The convict, Jean Valjean, played by Liam Neeson,
expecting punishment
for stealing, finds forgiveness and grace that brings him
transformational healing.

Three More Memorable Movies

For great drama, captivating mystery, during a time of
integration,
changing attitudes, and African American
transformation,
it surely won't bore you to see, *A Soldier's Story* (1984).
As a white man, it opened my eyes to the difficulty of
violating a code of racial secrecy,
to expose bigotry in the military. With a cast of tremen-
dous actors,
it casts thoughts on many factors.
Another movie I love to see, especially with my family, is
Beethoven (1992).
It cracked me up to see Dean Jones, always as a nice-guy,
who in light-weight roles did rely, now to comply
to portray a heavy. The dad's change creates
family-bonding,
with reluctant compromises, and progressively grants
him favor in his family's eyes.
I did winch at what a mess this canine beast could do,
yet for the dad, his love grew for pets and the rest
of his crew.
Selfish opportunistic goals gave way for family
values to stay.
A film about a pet fawn and a young boy, both to grow
close together,
and subliminally, in your heart, consider it your part and
see: *The Yearling* (1946).
If you ever wanted to check out if you had a heart
or just a stony thing, then watch the yearling.
I won't give away the ending, but I can't deny,

don't choose to see it
if you don't want to whimper and cry.
During an impoverished time, this boy,
to discover reality and coming of age,
journeys through a deep rite of passage.

A Few More Movie Moments

Any character actor would be chompin' at the bit to act
in the 1957 script of
12 Angry Men. I'm kind of "Fonda" of it. It would take a
total convergent verdict
for all to agree, yet only one had doubts about the
defendant being guilty. It
demonstrates: numbers against you don't count when
the persuasive logic
you bring wins out. Integrity uncompromised renders
prejudices' demise.
A movie about a family shaped by troubled times is
found in the 1994
Little Women. For girls to navigate an interested
potential mate,
amid sisters who can't always their interests relate;
interacting dynamics to impart,
yet truth comes by listening to one's own heart.
(Spoiler Alert—
don't read the next line if you've not seen the film) I
love the scene near the end,
when lost hope is discovered again, righting a lover's
misunderstanding. With this fella,
joy is seen when truth is revealed between he and Jo
under the umbrella.
If you love a good story set in the great outdoors,
showing human abuse
and nature's rebuke, I suggest, the 1988 film, *The Bear*.
An adult male grizzly does a turn-around, showing up in
fatherly-like fashion,

to a frightened needy cub's satisfaction. (Another spoiler alert is in the

following line. Decline to read it, if the film you've not seen).

It's amazing how the adult bear can refrain, not to inflict pain

but to show mercy, more than the man now begging weak in the knees,

who only could, previously, himself tease and taunt a helpless cub delightfully.

Last but not least is the 1965, black-and-white release, about a military prison to punish

army incorrigibles—*The Hill*. This drama wraps you in the emotion of the story

'til you wrestle with your own id and ego, and ask your-self, "What would I do?"

It reminds me that self-control is a fruit of the spirit, and a natural man needs a rebirth,

to become a doer of God's better plan. [50]

---

[50] I Corinthians 2:14

Remembering a Few More Movies

For all who love baseball, what can I say? Would one
decline to see *Field of Dreams*—
no way![51] There are so many spiritual corol-
laries to view:
faith versus reason, dare to dream versus secure living,
following the voice of the Spirit versus choosing to be
stuck in a regretful past.
Orchestration, seemingly, by the Divine Being taking
diverse persons who will pursue mystery's journey, each
better together than apart,
by following their own heart.
An old-fashioned film from much to glean, with a
romantic theme,
is *Marty*.[52] I watched it vicariously, placing myself in the
role of Marty,
opposite genteel girl, Clara. It's a story of two sensitive
people that meet;
a potentially great couple could they make. Yet, Marty's
lack of self-esteem
and insecurity, doubting he could be the man for this
good woman,
keeps you guessing. Will his lack of social skills, this
budding relationship kill?
Also, his male friends' peer pressure to be noncommittal,
hanging out as singles, is another questionable variable.

---

[51] *Field of Dreams*, 1989 (USA).

[52] *Marty*, 1955.

81

A fascinating movie I loved to see, and now acclaim: *The Imitation Game*. [53]

The undaunted challenge to break the German code with the enigma machine

took enduring will, so keen. The challenge of clashing egos had to be overcome.

It's really a war movie about an allied fight within the fight.

At the end of this film's story, I think that men never had more power

and the hardest decisions to make, concerning their fellow citizens' fate.

An aura of silence shrouds the outcome,

perhaps even as much as Truman's later decision on the A-bomb.

---

[53] *The Imitation Game*, 2014.

Chapter 5

My Take on Bible Stories

A Senior Tag Team [54]

It's not the proper action until the waiting and
responding.
Two faithful praying servants, by heartfelt purpose, were
led to bear
witness to "the reveal," the one, the Messiah of Israel.
Apparently,
a senior citizen who was near the end of his life; God
told Simeon
he would not die 'til he would see his Messiah arrive.
Following this same Spirit true, in God's timing, he came
into Jerusalem's temple.
Holding the child in his arms, he viewed these selected
two, Joseph and Mary,
to give consolation on their baby boy's first-born
dedication.
Simeon would speak to them of the impact of this Son
upon the Gentiles,
and the fall and rise of many in Israel. To them, God
would verify
the information with another Holy Spirit confirmation.
To Mary, the Lord God would prepare a mother's soul for
the worst,
yet foreshadowing Jesus's future purpose. Simeon
next foretold
of the Roman soldier's sword that would pierce Mary's
son's side
and remind her of this prophecy when He had died.
Another entered this scene: Anna, a widow of eighty-
four. This prophetess,

---

[54] Based upon Luke 2:25–38

a godly recluse, would also their boy's fate
substantiate—
that through this chosen Son would come redemption
to all who looked for it in Jerusalem. And these days,
all who love for His appearing look to Jerusalem skies,
uniting their natural with their spiritual eyes.

Freeing Acceptance [55]

When unfortunate fate needs an update, when you're
ostracized and criticized, when you
are part of a leprous group and must call from afar
to warn those more fortunate not to come near;
how can such a curse be reversed?
On Samaritan soil that day, ten men called to the one
who could free them from leprosy. No more socially
unacceptable evidence
would they display, as Jesus directed them to obey
the good and cleansing law of the priesthood.
As one traveled, he discovered he was healed on the way.
Great thankfulness drowned out any sense of
unworthiness.
He knew the lover of his soul totally accepted him.
Those who came to Jesus,
who ultimately would fulfill the law, in humility, were
received lovingly by Him, one
and all. Encountering Jesus, he discovered freeing
acceptance that day. No fear,
no timidity; only to return, falling to his knees, to give
Him glory.
This King had left home from heaven's comfort zone,
on a Fatherly mission to liberate those bound, entering
suffering mankind's realm.
No social caste system can last for certain
in the presence of the God who respects equally,
every person.
Jesus commended upon receiving thankful praise, from
a foreigner no less:

[55] Story found in Luke 17:11–19

why only did one return to give thanks? Through Him,
hasn't the Father welcomed us into His family? Can't we
return in thankfulness,
remembering when He totally heard our plea to take
our burdens
and give us His peace? Let's gather together our joy
to increase
in a spirited party! For He has taken our shame, being
Truth revealed,
and has truly set us free!

Clueless

Listening to the Bethel Music song, "God I Look to You" reminded me
of a miraculous story from Judah's history. [56] Three armies came upon Judah
to kill, steal, and plunder. But God stole their thunder.
Fearing the attack,
King Jehoshaphat, called his nation to a fast.
The king prayed in a new court before citizens coming from all around Judean towns.
His prayer would recall their God, so faithful. He reminded Jehovah
bold and loud, before the crowd, how God did forbid His chosen
when leaving Egypt for the Promised Land to attack these same peoples:
from Moab, Ammon, and Mount Seir. Now rendering evil for good,
they would appear, threatening in overwhelming numbers, creating fear.
King Jehoshaphat's prayer appealed to the God of Jacob, citing their weakness:
We have no power, these hordes to stand against. What to do? We don't have a clue.
But our eyes are upon You. Then came God-breathed inspiration. [57]

---

[56] 2 Chronicles 20

[57] 2 Timothy 3:16

A Word in due season, how sweet it is. [58] Direction and God's will came through the
prophecy of Jahaziel. He, moved by the Spirit, exclaimed, "Thus says the Lord to you: Do not be afraid nor dismayed, for the battle is not yours but God's."
Positioning themselves by simply standing still before their enemies,
they observed God is God over the crazies.
The attacking armies killed each other off.
All Judah would do, for the next three days: pick up their trophies.
Upon their soil, the "more-than-conquerors" received the spoils. [59]

---

[58] Proverbs 15:15

[59] Romans 8:37

Transformed

Where does one begin in a fallen world of sin? To doubt the supernatural
is the state of the natural. If I stick my hand in the fire, I will be burned.
To obey God takes an overcoming trust. Moses, staring at the rod
God told him to throw down, sees it has become another shape,
threatening him as a snake. Couldn't God change it back into a rod again?
Yet, not knowing, but to obey, Moses would pick up the serpent that day.
Didn't Jesus say His disciples would take up serpents?
The evil threatening that brings fear and harm to our mind,
and hidden poisons to drink would He thwart, for the gospel to go forth.
And aren't we to take up serpents, setting others free from our enemy? [60]
Those things that bring fears, striking us quickly as snakes, we can negate,
looking to Jesus, author of our faith. The serpent's sin in us becomes harmless brass: the
pole, a cross, in our wilderness. [61]
The disciples to obey filled the pots with water. How foolish they'd appear

---

[60] Mark 16:18

[61] John 3:14 (NKJV); Numbers 21:9

without the miracle. To obey His commands is to
take the risks
the natural mind rejects. The beautiful part; we also are
transformed
as we follow His heart. We go from faith to faith, the
developer in us to shape,
His kingdom come [62] And we, His members are part
of the sum!

---

[62] Romans 1:17 (NKJV); Hebrews 12:2 (NKJV); Luke 11: 2

Ruth[63]

As I read Psalm 31:19 the other day, I thought of Ruth,
choosing with Naomi to stay.
The verse read: "Oh how great is thy goodness, which
thou have laid up
for them that fear thee; which thou have
wrought for them
that trust in thee before the sons of men!" (KJV). [64]
I like to believe as truth, Naomi, the moth-
er-in-law of Ruth,
had demonstrated to this girl faith in the God of Israel.
Ruth, unlike her sister,
Orpah, chose not to stay behind, possibly marrying a cit-
izen of her own kind.
Though the loss of Naomi's husband and two sons
eroded even her pleasantries,
Ruth did see her deep need for loving company. Bitter as
Naomi claimed to be,
I believe Ruth knew her God's legitimacy. There was a
love our Caretaker placed in
Ruth's heart that kept her close to Naomi, never
to depart.
I can't improve on my favorite Bible book. Please for
blessings sake,
take a contemplative look. Oft quoted are Ruth's
words to Naomi:
"Entreat me not to leave thee, or to return from fol-
lowing after thee:

---

[63] This poem should be read in light of the Bible book of Ruth.

[64] Please excuse the King James Version. I chose it for its rhyme and
more generational feeling.

for whither thou goest, I will go; and where thou
lodgest, I will lodge:
thy people shall be my people and thy God, my God.
Where thou diest, will I die,
and there will I be buried: The Lord do so to me, and
more also,
if ought but death part thee and me" (KJV). You can
easily see,
upon reading Ruth's redemptive story, what Boaz
did for Ruth,
Christ did for His bride to be.

Inclusion

In the model prayer Jesus taught His disciples to pray,
He made inclusion linked to each and every man.
If we stay loyal to God's say, we forgive
everyone to expect
forgiveness from Him.[65] Doesn't that level the
"praying" field?
He will hear all who call on His saving Name without
casting any blame [66]
How did Jesus's teaching relate the value of a
sheep missing?
The ninety-nine, the shepherd left in open field to find
the one who'd wandered off.[67] How accountable
should we be
in the share of His care? I'm told that today in Midwest
farm country
when a child can't be found, community gather round
forming a hand-to-hand,
side-by-side chain, walking slowly across those fields of
grain. The wheat so tall
does for this tactic call. And, isn't that what we, as
Christ's body should do; He the head
calling us to prayer. We are His heart, His feet, His
hands, to implement
His saving plan, the child to apprehend.
The one word that images the biggest inclusion:
"whosoever,"

---

[65] Mark 11:25–26

[66] Romans 10:13

[67] Luke 15:4–7

whosoever would believe on Him, the ransom price paid for entry into

the Father's family would gain eternal freedom! Jesus chose death on that tree,

then committed himself to the grave, that unless, when He rose in victory,

we in victory could rise with Him. [68]

Secret Place

Did you ever feel the fear of harmful exposure? So much so, you wanted
to disappear? Did your strategy, so contrary to an accusing enemy,
declare to your heart, you'll be caught! Perhaps a brief stare, you mistook
for an exposing glare. You then discover, whether the cover remains hidden
or is blown, there's a secret place before His throne. [69] God's strong presence can lessen the blows of the gospel's foes. Jesus told Ananias,
Saul was chosen to suffer for His name's sake. Jesus's grace to Paul
He would not relent, for it was sufficient for every torment. [70]
Even a self-sworn curse by forty men, committed to kill Paul,
couldn't happen at all. God revealed the secret pact to Paul's nephew
to avert the attack.[71] Is the secret place only for a few to qualify? Isn't it for all
who depend upon our protector-God, so tall, under whose shadow fall? [72]
Doesn't this Author of life also hide His secret plans from His adversary?

---

[69] Hebrews 4:16

[70] Acts 9:16; 2 Corinthians 12:9

[71] Acts 23:20–24

[72] Psalm 91:2

Didn't Haman think Queen Esther was on his side,
to favor him
when a banquet to him and the king she did provide?
Yet, the God of Israel,
through Mordecai and her, united the Jews by fasting
and prayer. [73]
Didn't the powers that be succumb to the Redeemer's
plan on that wooden tree? [74]
We need not wrestle for control or power when
God reveals
the secret place in victory's hour. [75]

---

[73] Esther 5:10–12; 4:15–17

[74] 1 Corinthians 2:7–8

[75] Isaiah 54:17–18

Authority's Glory

Could we today, learn from David's Bible story? Hunted
as prey by King Saul,
he honored God's anointed king since
Saul was chosen as Israel's heritage prince. [76]
Under the prophet Samuel, led by God's Spirit,
Saul was sought out from all
the tribes of Israel.[77] Though Saul,
choosing his own way,
the Supreme Being to disobey, another king would
be chosen,
whose kingdom was not to depart, David,
a man after God's own heart. [78]
In direct opposition to God's sovereign will,
Saul with his 3,000 men pursued
David, to kill. One day in the desert of Engedi,
Saul, unknowingly, entered a cave
where David and his men did stay. He went in to
relieve himself,
yet David's men wanted to relieve David of him.
Standing down his men's plans,
David cut a corner from Saul's robe, healthily
allowing him
from the cave to go. To disarm the
fears of Saul, from a distance David to him, did call.
But, as proof he meant no harm to him,
David held up the cloth he'd cut. That day,

---

[76] 1 Samuel 10:1

[77] 1 Samuel 10:20–21

[78] 1 Samuel 13:13–14

even Saul would proclaim David's integrity and
acknowledge him as Israel's chosen future king. [79]
Again, Saul's inner strife
would drive him to seek David's life. David would
in remembrance write
about when his enemies so near: "The Lord is my light
and my salvation;
whom shall I fear?"[80] A spy would reveal to David, as
the light of a lamp,
the whereabouts of Saul's camp. Again, sneaking up on
Saul and his sleeping men,
he did forbid the taking of his life, even for all that he
did. His water jug and spear
would be taken. The next day from mountain to moun-
tain, David would cry out
across the divide, holding up Saul's jug and spear to see,
showing him his mercy.
Though Saul spoke a blessing over David that day, the
end of that king's story
didn't bring God glory.[81] A lesson from David's story:
Can we honor
our nation's leader? Can we not disgrace his special
authorized place,
and can we let God decide when our leader to replace?

---

[79] 1 Samuel 24:1–20

[80] Psalm 27:1

[81] 1 Samuel 26 (NKJV); 31:1–7

Whatever the Call

This man could not stand tall, seeing himself a sinner
before a Holy God.
He realized his speech unclean would betray him as a
spokesman for
the one supreme. Once God's flying creature with the
cleansing ember
would touch his defiled lips, he would give more than
lip service.
Changed by the altar coal, he surrendered, heart and
soul.[82] This mere man
would speak, hidden for centuries, redemption's plan.
Can we imagine his dedication; declaring God's
Word to those
who'd stopped hearing? [83] Looking back, I think
we'd agree,
the Messiah, Yeshua, Isaiah would decree. Just take a
gander at Isaiah,
chapter fifty-three. He warned his nation to turn
from insincere
offerings for sin, with no repentance to begin. His words
about fasting,
when enacted, bring change impacting. [84]
In Isaiah's faithful loyalty, he would have chances
to speak for
both the Jew and the Greek and you and me
hopeful prophecy.

---

[82] Isaiah 6:1–8

[83] Isaiah 6:9–10

[84] Isaiah 58

The Messiah's calling would be heard in the synagogue, when Jesus,
with gracious sound, would read them in His hometown. [85]
And, a hope to birth, for nation Israel, would flow forth, from words
Isaiah spoke for this future earth. [86]

---

[85] Isaiah 61:1–2; Luke 4:18–19

[86] Isaiah 61:8–11

Dead Man Walking

There's something to be said about Paul, himself to deny,
for he chose daily to die.[87] Spiritually speaking, he took
his death with
Christ on the cross very seriously.[88] He knew dead men
don't sin,
so each day to begin he reckoned himself dead to sin! [89]
However, what was the physical side that
ignored pride and
kept him in the Spirit's stride, free from defection.
Wasn't it his belief in Christ, the Resurrection? He wrote
to the church in Corinth
of his troubles in Asia. He did have a great start
at Lystra,
for he, perceiving a crippled man's faith when he
did preach,
commanded this man to his feet. Yet, the crowd
stood in awe,
only to him laud, thinking, *he must be a god!*
And, who would show up on the spot—the persecuting
Jews from the team's last spot.
This time they would succeed. Citizens would see
Paul bleed,
not a god, only a man, as they stoned him, leaving him
for dead. After,
his body on the ground, the disciples would
gather round.

---

[87] 1 Corinthians 15:31

[88] Galatians 2:20

[89] Romans 6:11

How close to death was the apostle that day? It seems,
in all likelihood,
the disciples did pray. The day after his stoning,
returning to the city,
the people would stop their talking, their eyes
opening wide.
For them, they saw a dead man walking.[90]

---

[90] Acts 14:5, 8–20

The Importance of Water Baptism

The life of Jesus tells us that He knew what the
Pharisees knew too—
that He baptized even more than the prophet John,
though not He,
but His disciples He relied upon.[91]
John's life story tells us that masses from
Jerusalem, Judea,
Samaria, and around Jordan, (comprising a vast area)
repented of their sins
to be baptized by Him.[92] When I compared these
two truths,
I realized the larger view, movies don't include, what
the Bible alludes to:
that Jesus's disciples worked laboriously to bring
God glory.
Today, many devout Muslims believe that for one of
them Islam to leave
by Christian water baptism is an intolerable sin.
Doesn't that speak to the power that baptism
does within?
What about the first Pentecost after the cross?
One hundred twenty disciples were prepared that day,
when 3,000 they baptized to follow THE WAY?
What a water-works of joy happened, a labor of love,
experiencing a many salvation at that blessed
location! [93]

---

[91] John 4:1–2

[92] Matthew 3:5

[93] Acts 2:41

And, it's importance at that site, for the baptizers must
have increased,
along with their physical and spiritual appetite.
May God's Holy Spirit be poured out anew,
on Middle East Gentile and Jew. [94]

---

[94] Acts 2:38, 17

Parallel Promise

Was there a need for my faith to be built to envision
God's will for me complete?
When reading certain scriptures my mind would go tilt.
OK, I can believe
that God predestined me. But, to be as His son Jesus, in
this world,[95] to me,
would take such divine conformity.[96] Yet, God asked
rhetorically,
"Is there anything too hard for Me?" [97]
Though in a parallel promise illustrated in nature, Jesus
spoke of a tiny seed,
to grow into a plant, then into a tree.[98] He told us to
have this kind of faith. [99]
What does a mustard seed believe? Doesn't it just
depend on God to become a tree?
One of the reasons, when my wife and I were house
hunting we could both agree,
Father God gave us the same strong peace. And among
many reasons:
the backyard tree. You see, it's a huge oak to
remind me also
of the parallel of natural growth. Thus, the saying:
"From an acorn to an oak."

---

[95] 1 John 4:17

[96] Romans 8:29

[97] Jeremiah 32:27

[98] Matthew 13:32

[99] Matthew 17:20

Could this Creator, who spoke all into existence
with a word,
help us so small, conform to the image of our Lord? [100]
When you live with yourself each day, spiritual growth
can seem slow, almost
unobservable. A reminder from your past can, for sure,
make you laugh or cringe about
your former immature self. It's the gardener's job to tend
to the vine.
Our job is to in Him abide.

---

[100] Romans 12:2

Extravagant Love Received

Our selfless Lord prepared each day for ministry, up before sun's break to pray.
His desire: to put Father's Love on display. One day He was invited for dinner, as a guest, to risen Lazarus's address.
While at the table, his friend Mary came in.
By her luxurious action, others judged it a sin.
Breaking a costly container of fragrant oil, she then poured the ointment
on Jesus in affectionate stages. The cost of the lotion, a working man's yearly wages.
Objections arose, why the waste of this costly oil? The case was made,
Jesus heard told, for ministry to the poor this gift could have been sold.
Still, Jesus loved her lavish gift and welcomingly received it.
He reminded all, you'll always have the poor, but you'll not always have Me.
Showing His humanity, He honored individual worth, while in His divinity, received worship's love while on this earth.
And, an example He set by accepting thankfully her act of love without regret.
He promised in memory to bless this Mary who chose the best part,
by totally following her heart. [101]

---

[101] Based on Mark 14:3–9; John 12:1–8

Desert Delight!

Enslaved, feeling hopeless, heavy burdened; then,
two men show up to say, God sent them.
Moses with Aaron performed signs confirming
unto His chosen ones, these brothers He did send. [102]
Temporarily, the Hebrews' hopes arose, while to Pharaoh
Aaron and Moses would go.
What demand would God Almighty place
upon that man?
"Let My people go!"
The reason for the release: God wanted to meet them
for a wilderness feast. [103]
They were to have a time of worship and celebra-
tion, dancing,
a taste of freedom with the King of heaven.
Though Pharaoh's heart was hardened, the pride inside
led to selfish insistence and resistance
to forewarned harbingers of Adonai's consequen-
tial dangers.
Ten plagues Egyptians would suffer. And Jehovah
would have His people's feast. They would eat,
while the death angel would see the lambs' blood-
marks on their
abodes when he would pass over. Egypt's leader brought
destruction
on his people's lands and homes; they became
deeply forlorn

---

[102] Exodus 4:1–8

[103] Exodus 5:1

at the loss of each firstborn.[104]
Yet, El-Shaddai set the Hebrews free.
That holy day they ate and fled, having been
favored and blessed by the indigenous Egyptians. [105]
They would seemingly find
themselves trapped with their backs to the Red Sea,
chased by Pharaoh and his army.
God would finally have His way that day. For they
walked across on dry land,
a release of power by the rod in Moses's hand.
Though the children of God would cross on dry
ground; in a covering of water, the following pursuers
would drown.
On victory's side, the desert delight would abound! In
joy they did shout!
They sang the song of Moses. Miriam got her timbral,
the women following her out. The Hebrews danced
about, twirling and shouting that
night with desert delight! [106]

---

[104] Exodus 12:1–14

[105] Exodus 12:36

[106] Exodus 14:9–15:21

A Godly Repayment Plan[107]

Here's a story that brings the God of mercy glory! God,
who sees all,
revealed to His man in Israel, like a spy-cam, the Syrian
army's plans.
Everywhere the Syrian military planned a sur-
prise attack,
Israeli intelligence did not lack. For God would let His
prophet Elisha know
what is what; and Israel's king through Elisha would
learn of the thing.
The Syrian king came to know, for their intelli-
gence-gathering eventually did show;
the agent told his king, for as soon as you speak a thing,
even in your bedroom,
God's prophet will know. Asking, where is this man, he
was told, Dothan!
Upon surrounding that city with a vast army, Elisha's
servant viewed
in fear the Syrian forces, asking Elisha "What
shall we do?"
His reply, "Do not fear, for those who be with us are
more than be with them."
In a short prayer, Elisha's request opened the ser-
vant's eyes.
The servant could clearly see, faith to inspire,
God's massive army that day with chariots of fire.
As Syrian forces descended, another of Elisha's
arrow-prayers

---

[107] 2 Kings 6:8–23

would strike the enemy with blindness, and Elisha
would not to be seen.

Using deception as a weapon, for they could not take a
peek, Elisha misdirecting,

telling them he'd lead them to the right city where this
prophet could be found,

their plan to confound.

Keeping pace, he led them
to the Samarian place
where they met up with the king of Israel.

The Lord opened the eyes of these men to reveal they
were indeed,

captured by the army of Israel. Israel's king, submitting
to heaven's authority,

asked of Elisha reverently, "My father, should I kill
them?" Elisha's answer that day

truly displayed God's mercy. The king would prepare a
great feast

of food and drink. And after, he would send them away
home to their master,

to convey: we were had, but it didn't turn out so bad.

It brought no more raiding bands, for some time on
Israel's lands,

their farmers to reap the harvests of their hands.

To Differ

Have you ever felt pressured by peers for you to meet
their anticipated deadline?
Of course, what they have for you in mind is not always
true. In this case,
Jesus's brother's advice—how to be the miracle worker
from Galilee in the metro city.
Was their jealousy like that, that each son had toward
Joseph in Jacob's clan?
Had they not known the anger and hate that could
await his fate at the seat of religion
in Jerusalem? They reasoned, perhaps, if you're really
God's special son,
who will save us from our sins, go to the city of the
great king, and do your thing,
so *all* your disciples can see. With his life they were
willing to toss the dice.
They may have thought, what opportunity he
had lost; what impact he could make, with
seven days of this feast to take, the popu-
lace to seal, performing so many miracles to
heal. He's just piddling around in his prayer
shawl, demonstrating no clout, choosing
with his God
to hide out.
Jesus's reply to them could be a warning to you and me,
and to all who seek to blend in.
They hate Me because I reveal this world's sin. Your
time is now.

He, in faith, may have thought,
I'll pave THE WAY.
They will understand on their salva-
tion day. [108]

---

[108]   based upon John 7:1–9

Two Words

Two words, if only I could imbue them like post-its
before my mind
for all time. They would transform my life's attitude.
They are: "as unto."
How could I half-heartedly do so many things, lacking
respectful quality?
I know there's forgiveness to receive and then
to move on.
But aware of those two words; I could prepare the
offering of my heart
and hands, for my Redeemer and Friend, worthy so of
all glory.
I will agree with God's decree—"Commit your works
(as) unto Me
and your thoughts will be established."[109] For in
all my ways,
first and not last, I'll acknowledge Him that He will
direct my paths.[110]
Anointed for good grace's goal-end, "doing service
(as) unto the Lord and not to men." [111]
For if we seek every moment to please our King,
we will with hearty exuberance properly treat each pre-
sented thing,
knowing it's not laboring for the pay that passes away
but "as unto" the Lord that brings the lasting reward. [112]

---

[109] Proverbs 16:3

[110] Proverbs 3:6

[111] Ephesians 6:7

[112] Colossians 3:23

Chapter 6

Perspectives, Some with, Some Without Scripture

Perspectives

Us—Are we falsely confident, united, one and all,
though the raft
we are on is reaching a dangerous waterfall?
Should we have
heeded the river's warning signs along the way
and stopped
at the boater's dock? Fortunately, though our raft was
destroyed that day,
our lives He did save.
Them—Look at those fools ignoring the high
water's flow,
taking lightly the increasing cautions to stop, further
not to go.
They laughed at us in pride, considering our truth a lie.
Now, from the banks' safety, we spy. Perhaps collectively,
we'll watch them die.
Him—Though many, my Truth ignore, others will
find gladness
in heavenly river's flow.[113] Never take pleasure,
or in spite,
harden your hearts to those who deride.[114] Give them
My saving name to call out.
Lament and weep for those who don't turn about. [115]
For those whose choice is to turn to My way, rejoice
always with those who rejoice. [116]

---

[113] Psalm 46:4; John 7:38

[114] 1 Corinthians 13:6

[115] Luke 13:34

[116] Philippians 4:4; Luke 15:10

Me—Now, looking back I can view each group I
relate to.
God's unfailing pursuit broke through to reveal
Jesus, true.
Now, as a follower, in His place, He begs me,
show others God's mercy and grace.

Whose Term Is It?

There's a phrase that either sounds an alarm or
gives a hope to explore a certain promising person more.
Depending on the speaker and the situation,
the term carries a positive or negative connotation.
When hearing this phrase, like a mail-sorter,
your mind does file the expression in the proper order.
The public alarm sounds within when a police commis-
sioner calls someone
"a person of interest." Then again, after a businessman
conducts an interview,
and thinks to himself, "a person of interest"
in the situation, the hope to fulfill the need
brings elation.
How about compatibility on a matching online website;
"a person of interest" might be just right. Shouldn't we
ask ourselves,
what sort of person of interest are we? And,
where should the interest others see in me lead?
For me, I'd just like to introduce you to my best friend,
to step aside while in His friendship you may abide.
For, the person of interest He is,
will reveal the great interest true He has in you. [117]

---

[117]   John 3:16

Nature's Call, the Lure of Agur

Seeking to understand, in nature we can see God's
Hand. According to Truth's Book,
we are expected to know there's a Creator when at
nature, we look. [118]
The observations of Agur reveal, intrinsic, instinctive
mysteries, the Maker did conceal:
Agur meditates on animal behavior, questioning a
deeper meaning. Examples
indicate movements designed to overcome nature's
resistance to each animal's
insistence. These noble examples should we, at times
follow, our regal character to
evoke: the lion, the greyhound, and the goat.[119] Agur,
being a naturalist, adds some small
creatures with innate "wisdom" to his list. The ant's dili-
gence does a lazy man convict,
while demonstrating the protestant ethic explicit. The
rock hydrax,
though soft and furry, in their "ingenious way" make
their homes in the rock's crag.
And the locusts, with no king to lead, in "perfect forma-
tion" and synchronization,
fly to the sky. What of the spider's evasive design? The
multidirectional,

---

[118] Romans 1:20
[119] Proverbs 30:30–31

lightweight, arachnid could be found in your place
or mine. [120]
Without scientific inquiry, I can easily see how one
would wonder
how the eagle soars so effortlessly. Measuring wind
speed's flow by man,
under its wings we know the eagle's "plan," waiting to
catch nature's gift,
the air's uplift. Now that we know its muscles and
scales purpose,
the snake displays how it can move on an
uneven surface.
Sailors, bouncing over waves can make them wonder
the way of a ship on the sea's water. When the tug and
pull of emotions flow,
who can know the outcome of a guy and girl? [121]

---

[120] Proverbs 30:28—The Hebrew word in Strong's Concordance refers to a lizard or a spider. The lizard is probably more fitting, but I chose the spider for poetic flow.

[121] Proverbs 30:18–19

Unhandled Disappointment

Have you ever had your life on hold? Perhaps not
life or death
but your life bereft? The more unfilled a longing, the
more your heart for it
is pining. Especially if you've been given a promise of its
soon coming,
then prolonged, so you've wondered, is it to delay the
bad news you've pondered?
If it's a thing you perceive will bring your life
greater validity,
you yearn to see the prize when it does arrive.
Is it all I waited for or a different material,
shape, or size?
Maybe the one in the store, not quite a perfect fit, you
chose to send off for.
When you went to the store brand's website, you viewed
more variety.
But the pictures to see didn't match delivery's reality.
The online in-stock claim, now you mistrust and say,
why the delay?
Another glitch, upon arrival what I longed to try on
was switched.
The clothing, you marked on the online form, your
appearance to enhance,
had little resemblance. Maybe another time, you
searched and searched to find
something for a special need to meet. Upon delivery,
you see it wouldn't do.
Now it's your turn to mail it back, paying postage too.
If you've lost your peace and blurted out language amiss,

be quick to ask the Lord's forgiveness. For this was a lost chance to, in everything, give thanks. [122]

In

I ask myself, how do I make this transition, from in, to
out, and then, in again?
No, it's not location. It's mental persuasion. Can I
be myself,
whether alone or in company? One way,
I've decided, though I've failed before at several tries:
I'll avoid hot-button issues that lead to a rut in adamant,
angered thinking.
Not that I'm a coward, but to flow with the
spirit of peace,
I'll move forward, hopefully toward where the Prince of
Peace agrees.
Now, back to the transition—Outside I will be myself,
when I speak as a citizen of
heaven, like a migrant passing through a country's land,
listening to
the Spirit true, not fixed upon a traditional worldview.
Now, "in" again,
I'll be like a football quarterback, wise to call an audible.
The set positions of my mind do a paradigm shift,
negating oppositions' trained thinking.
Also, those looking for workable gains, can learn from
my creative Coach,
for I'm listening within this helmet of hope He gave me,
His callings wiser than you or I could foresee.
I then, from "in-time" spent with Him, can be who He's
told me to be.
Sometimes, it's not going out at all. It's just a phone call,
sending a letter or a card, a text, or planning an act
of kindness.

Then, I go out with authority, trusting His instructions
will personify this identity, though for now, in a some-
what shaky body.
After, upon His personal review, alone with
Him, the love,
grace, and corrective truth will thrill me through
and through
'til the next game plan we'll do. Of course, life is
not a game.
Yet I know executing His plan for me is refining and
defining my true identity. [123]

---

[123] Romans 12:2

Waking Up Thankful

I awoke after a good sleep. Even before a worry I
could reject,
an expression came from my heart I knew not to neglect.
Thank you for remembering me. In all the things
You tend to,
thank you for including me. In love, in word, in
deed; indeed,
thank you for remembering me. Even when I forget
that always
You are with me, that to You I can call or plea for aid I
need; thank you, for
remembering me. Even giving thanks for the nature
around me,
I can see You designed me into Your ecology. If I were
not thankful,
it would have been a first step to embark into incip-
ient dark. [124]
A car cannot run on empty. Spiritually, I oft forget to
say each day,
"Fill me up," You look out for me. You send reminders
that point me on Your way, providing rest areas on each
traveling highway
and byway. Thank you for faithfully remembering me.
I love you gratefully. Your example inspires an ele-
vated thought—
it's been a quite a while since I've bought a pack of
"thank you" cards.
I'll follow-up giving thanks to You, by thanking
those I've

---

[124] Romans 1:21

received blessings through. Their goodness, too,
reminds me of You. In thanking them, with
note and pen,
I'll give a lengthened extension, in thanking you.

The Other Foot

Have You heard an expression and never considered,
with it, the picture given,
For instance, the saying: "Now the shoe's on the
other foot"
I assumed this adage somehow meant a reversal new,
something about, getting back at you.
However, can your picture standing with a right shoe on
your left foot,
or even more awkward, both shoes uncomfortably,
although providing symmetry,
toes pointing out, while cramped within each shoe,
the opposite bend for your toes to go. Was the wearer of
comfortable shoes
forced to swap with a person who wore his shoes on his
feet opposite?
I get that it had something to do with the one having
the advantage,
gaining new perspective from the one who had not.
Could it mean the one accustomed, the other, to
step upon,
now has the heavy boot that looms over them?
Could it mean
this one should have seen, all along, the lower
one's view
and extended mercy and grace, as was his abled place?
And when the downtrodden finds reversal's superior
loftier triumph,
will they embrace, "Do unto others as you would have
them do unto you?" [125]

---

[125] Luke 6;31 (NLT)

Just a thought—Did China's cultural revolution
of '66–'76
lead to a reversal of fortune? Did white- and blue-collar
jobs reversal,
Mandarin language for China universal, smug-
gled Bibles,
and underground Christians humble, yet with
persecution
promised, increase heaven's feast for many from
the East? [126]

---

[126] 2 Timothy 3:12; Matthew 8:11

Widening the Narrow

I've been thinking about balance and confidence lately.
I'm amazed and dazed
at gymnasts, athletes, high-wire acts, and spring-
board troupes
on *Ed Sullivan Show* repeats, when witnessing
their feats.
I wonder, how many hours of practice it must
have taken for the flawless to replace any mistakes.
I notice a tightrope isn't quite as narrow when perfect
balance is invoked
and confidence becomes stoked. There's a good word
from a proverb: the way of the lazy
man is like a hedge of thorns, but the way of the upright
is a highway (NKJV),
or, as the Amplified Bible would say: but the way [of
life] of the upright
is smooth and open like a highway."[127] And for widening
the narrow way
that Jesus spoke of, a key is found in Proverbs 16:17a—
"The highway of the upright is to depart from evil." [128]
I look at the conditioned competition on *America
Ninja Warriors.*
They do it primarily to be the best they can be. Why, as
Christians should we not want
the same and by His Hand train? We are to
seek His fame,

---

[127] Proverbs 15:19

[128] Matthew 7:13–14 (implied from KJV)

bringing honor to His name. Even the well-trained winners would admit:
they prepared, but His grace added strength to succeed above their expectancy.
Many believers will not be in the limelight, yet for their faithfulness,
the Lord will, on them, shine His light that day,
when rewards await those who obey. [129]
Acting in harmony as members of His body, by His grace many
will enjoy forever heaven's family in the Father's company.

---

[129] 2 Corinthians 5:10

Excavating Breakthrough

Have you ever been to a celebration that honors others
for their dedication?
Did it seem too long for you? Perhaps that was a good
thing too.
What if you had a daughter or son slated to receive
recognition?
Didn't others sit in their chairs while we waited
for the name
we sought to hear? Wouldn't one of those who built
Jerusalem's wall,
when kudos were read, have been pleased to hear their
name's call? [130]
When we rejoice with those who rejoice, especially
as a whole,
we find patience and unity to enthrall.
What if you discovered honorable ancestors in your
family tree?
God wants to honor those that honored Him. [131]
Joseph and Mary would have been encouraged to see,
together, each's genealogy.[132] Exploring can sometimes
seem boring.
Yet, ask a miner whether a non-yielding load was
worth exploring
when he finally found a vein of gold? So, dig through
those lists 'til you find those
nuggets that enrich. Hidden in an Israeli family tree,

---

[130]   Nehemiah, Chapter 3

[131]   John 12:26

[132]   Matthew 1:1–25; Luke 3:23–37

we find a great story. A prayer answered for this man
can be a prayer
answered for you and me—Jabez. [133]
God felt his pain and gave this righteous seeker
great gain.
So, read really slow or listen audible
for hidden treasure, for it's a kingly thing to search out
a matter. [134]

---

[133] 1 Chronicles 4:9–10

[134] Proverbs 25:2

The Spider's Gift

Better than fictional E. B. White's spider, spelling out
praises for Wilbur, [135]
real life spiders spin threads like silken steel.
Commercial applications beyond Peter Parker [136]
expectations,
this nature spider's thread stretches our imaginations:
to be used in wear-resistant, lightweight clothing,
and still,
over time will look "as good as new." There are
implications
involving surgical operations, used for artificial liga-
ments and tendons,
in seatbelts to hold you fast, or in parachutes, your
life to last.
Should your wounds accrue, find it in bandages and sur-
gical thread too.
Then in rope, it's used to pull heavy loads and to rescue.
Its tensile strength will even take a bullet for you.
Defenders invest, in this life-saving vest.
Perhaps I should have entitled this poem: "Ode to
the Spider,"
but then for strengthening applications,
I should give an equal turn, to our friend, the silkworm.

---

[135] *Charlotte's Web*, E. B. White, Oct. 12, 1952.
[136] *Spider-Man*, the movie, 2002.

To Never Let Go

A shared love, like a father with his son, or a mother
with her daughter,
only could be understood by another who experienced
the blessing
after uniting again with the one who had been missing.
The safety of home and family, pulled like a rug out
from under thee;
how cannot such a fall bring shock to the assumed good,
on the comfortable spot, where that one stood?
The truth becomes discovered by youth in saying:
"You don't know what you've got 'til it's been taken."
Sin's cost has robbed innocence with self-persona's loss.
Where could you safely vent all the hurt you lament?
Who can relate to the shame and regret that plague you?
Only one who has been there too.
And, what if another could eliminate all the harm done?
What if you could start over, knowing from hindsight
not to listen to those misleading voices and make
destructive choices?
What friend could you confide in, to be there, per-
fectly aware,
and give you wise, guiding counsel? And, if that one
and the same
could bestow forgiveness, rendering a verdict of
not guilty?
For this God-sent friend, by divine plan, paid in fact,
the price for even your most hateful, deliberate act
to erase shame's blame, His own foretold life loss,
on a calculated hilltop cross? [137]

---

[137] Isaiah 53; I Peter 2:24

Conversely

Because our natural minds need to be refined, under-
standing to impact,
may more easily come with this tact:
look at the converse of scripture verse.
For example, if without faith we can't please God,
to please Him what would it take?
And, if we see that faith works by love, what would faith
to please God need
for you and me? If God is love, how would we describe
what He cannot be?
Sometimes thinking the opposite brings positivity.
Perhaps you could rewrite 1 Corinthians 13:4–8 in this
darkened light.
Those who lack love are impatient and mean. They
begrudge the
others' likeabilities, for in the spotlight they crave to be.
They, in pretense, flaunt their importance. They
trample others
to get their own way and distort truth to inject a lie,
forcing themselves first between the divide.
They will heap self-praise, pumping themselves up,
like inflated, oversized,
prized tires, while deflating the air of worth in faithful
followers.
They are easily upset by an alternate viewpoint,
perceived as a threat, though only another's opinion was
expressed.
They rejoice to see hopes dashed in others who seek to
become true lovers.

The Outspoken Broken

The unspoken thumbs clicking in spirit unity at the
"open mic" poetry speak,
says we're with you, brother, with you, sister. It may be
a complaint,
a deep hole from which one bares the soul.
It may be a pregnant burst of emotional stress delivered
forth in catharsis.
The speaker's beginning uncertainty grows stronger with
each emotional plea.
Hear me! Help's cry cries out, please get me!
It might not seem to make sense. It may just be a protest
against life's hardness,
like when bacon crackles on a hot grill, spitting multidi-
rectional as it shrivels.
After, each poem the listeners applaud the gutsy
guy or gal
who made themselves so vulnerable. Will he or she, in
love's need,
surrender to an attractive admirer for tempo-
rary pleasure?
Or, will they have learned from past encounters how
broken by misuse even leads to self-abuse?
There's only one who surely loves purely, and can
bring clarity,
replacing a life of misery.
A dashed hope is found,
resurrected in Jesus, His name to call upon!
For He came in unselfish love's mission.

Mistaken Identity

This girl smiled; eyes wide at me. Overcome by
her beauty,
I quickly thought, *what warranted such a welcoming*
appearance so unearned by me?
I tried to hide my surprise and modified my
return greeting
in such a way as to not scare her away.
Did she know me from somewhere?
Should I ask her? Should I dare?
Pretending to have lost my bearing I looked around.
I actually peered to see if another recipient
could be found.
I hoped she meant me, dispelling this fantasy.
Closing in swiftly came her family: a sister, a brother,
college-age friends greeting one another.
I noticed she greeted all in her special, kind-hearted way,
her goodness and inner beauty showing through.
Realizing then, *though she was special too,*
I was experiencing her in You.

Forever

Forever is a long, long, long time.
It's like staring at the repeat button's letter, printed out
when held down.
It's more than the human race,
exchanging batons for every light-year race in space.
It's more than contemplating His supreme thoughts
toward me,
as numerous as the grains of sand, then adding each
person's, collectively.
Is it linear, like an entity traveling that never wears out,
or is it cyclical, regenerating itself?
How many dimensions does it contain, and is it true?
You're the one by which all things consist.
Are they held together by divine will? In this vastness
could a God be so personal to have us in mind?
If so, how would He reveal Himself in such a way
as to say:
respond to My love in childlike faith,
you'll never comprehend Me anyway.

Override

From before man, it's evident God had His sovereign plan.
God of free will knew Lucifer would become the father of lies,
that mankind would disobey His only command;
for redemption Jesus would have to die.
Yet, in each present now, I picture the designer like an aircraft flyer,
saying, Let's switch from automatic to override.
I see in relationship with man, a safety backup plan
by design, influencing God Himself to change His mind.
Aren't we created in His image? Cannot sin's affrontery
make Him angry? The golden calf, His chosen did make,
idolatry not to forsake, angered Him, emotions to
consume them with the sin He did hate.
Yet, safety's design built into His plan allowed Moses to plea and reason,
to spare his fellowman. Adonai would change His mind that day,
demonstrating Himself the God of mercy. [138]
I think of those I care for. I, before, was like those who
spit in the face of this pure Savior. Yet, from the wooden tree, He,
with shortened-breath, forgave you and me.
Now, I can pray in faith for those whose lives
insult His ways,
and know, the Holy Spirit's wisdom can save a soul.

---

[138] Exodus 32:8–14 (NKJV).

All Out

Don't you know, a fish out of water is much easier to
pull to land
on the bank or in a boat. It, dangling on your line's play,
has no chance to get away. You can collect the catch
with a net, yet, swinging it in, you can grab the leader
to detach.
Christians at sporting events with well-meaning, seek to
draw viewers in
by holding signs of John 3:16. Many have seen and even
read the verse
but have not understood what the word *believe* would
convey in Jesus's day.
To Nicodemus, He spoke; it would invoke a call of deep
faith in the Son of God.
The Classic Amplified Bible edition seeks to identify the
"whosoever" position;
giving clarity to receive insight for "believe,"—to rely on,
trust in, and cling to.
To my sign-holding, life-saving friends with good
intentions,
I suggest a clearer invitation to the lost, both for the
mind and for the heart
to count the cost—Luke 9:23–24. For the one who
would come after Me, Jesus did say,
will take up his cross daily and follow Me.
This newcomer would not choose to save his life in
this world,
but for Jesus' sake, their life to lose.
For the analogy of a fish, I must admit,

I wasn't the hook-line-and-sinker kind. Had I jumped
high to find,
that well-cast fly, I declare, I'd have struggled less in
nothing but air.
Then I'd have known my cross to bear. He did manage
to pull me in,
but netted me in the watery environment,
I used to fight Him. In His strength I discovered my
weakness. He did wear me down,
and within His will and purpose, me He did surround.
Had I known more of what I was
getting into, for heaven's sake, for that matter,
I'd have offered myself on this King's platter.

Enjoying the Moment

At the supermarket, I watched with glee to see
a boy of about five leave his mother's side
in a flash to the weight scale. His mom affirms a
weight gain;
the boy, happy to hear his progress so far this year.
An earlier scene, the same store; a mother with daughter
of about four,
the mother, stepping on the scale, her little girl seeing
the needle spring,
clapped and jumped excitedly with delight at the nee-
dle's new height.
Looking back, I viewed a picture from my youth,
a birthday party with five boys dressed like cowboys.
To be Roy Rodgers or Gene Audrey; at least we wanted
to be the good guys.
Yet lacking fixed hope, none became cowpokes.
Our world was the now, not the future.
Why not enjoy the present moment while it's
young and fun?
To be content sometimes it's best shutting out all but
the moment.

Inlay

One of the beauties I've seen is wood with inlay.
Perhaps different stains or different woods or same stain
but combining shades and hues of beauty.
The grains may flow like rain, direction the same,
perhaps diagonal to horizontal but drawing us to
the center,
unifying both skill and treasure.
Another crafted endeavor: dovetail.
Dovetail fits a ninety-degree assembly of
cemented strength
with puzzle accuracy. Another dovetail—the Bible says,
"The evening and the morning were the first day."
A night and a morning dovetailed from dark to light,
to see more clearly, bringing hope from heaven's height.
How about folks like me, who embrace the
night to party?
We just need to plan with next-day in mind,
not to our bodies be unkind.
For tomorrow is tonight's birthday,
and tomorrow's birthday is tonight,
when we go from dark to light.

The Pile of Plenty

Walking near a business, I almost overlooked a pile
of plenty—
acorns formed a pile near a parking lot curb. I thought,
no squirrels to gather,
like those acorns scattered under my backyard tree.
No squirrels to traverse the frequent traffic for win-
ter's storage.
What about the world's foods? People need to
spread them:
a disparity of plenty and the lack of many. It's
a changing,
ongoing problem to solve, greater than man's resolve.
Tariffs, sanctions, wars, genocide, and greed hinder
reaching those in need.
I'm praying for peace, like the serenity you see in a peo-
ple-friendly park.
Should not children be free to play, not to worry of
arsenal munitions today?
The irony of children with bloated tummies, yet
near starving?
Let's move that pile of plenty and seek lives to save
worldwide.
World leaders, please agree for posterity's sake, homes
and lands not to vacate,
disrupting education and prosperity; let truth's
freedom liberate.
I pray each one would see a reflection of them in the
families of man.
Just as slavery was abolished here over a century and a
half ago, it took a costly fight,

many lives sacrificed to obtain that right. Though
God's answer
I long to be sooner than later, I appeal to His nature, I
implore Him,
His Word of promise to secure
"I am the Lord who exercises kindness, justice and
righteousness on earth, for in these I delight."
declares the Lord. [139]

---

[139] Jeremiah 9:24 NLT (paraphrased by author)

An Unjust Comparison

The natural mind jumps to demote or promote one by
unjust comparison.
The gift to us won't be seen without the inner self
coming out.
A heart of faith or doubt won't be evident 'til the mouth
speaks it out.
We often compare people on an unjust scale. As the
author C. S. Lewis's[140]
example: Two people, we should not compare, for this
present, the past they did bear.
Dick Firkin is so likeable, kind, considerate, friendly.
Miss Bates, no so, but what of origins?
Mr. Firkin hasn't changed much since his proper social
upbringing.
Miss Bates abruptly turned around; responding when
the Savior's voice did sound.
You don't dismiss the one under the Master's hand of
construction.
Tis better to engage with the one in whose image
you're made,
than continue in another established way.
A good father doesn't allow a neighbor to discipline his
son or daughter,
or social media for that matter.
His love covers immature mistakes,
the wrong choices they make,
'til loyalties seen, gather truths into trust.

---

[140] *Mere Christianity*—C. S. Lewis, 1952, renewed 1980.

It's Outside Your Door

I heard a phrase that opened to me thoughts of
possibilities.
The phrase—"The store outside your door."
Nature's food source,
that's taking us back to
ancestors we thought primitives
but now we make medicine derivatives—
plants, roots, seeds, shoots, etc.; all kinds of
hidden treasures, in which now we revisit their lore:
"the store outside your door."
Even now, a new chapter unfolds.
Harvesters explore the ocean floor.
Nodules of combined metal deposits,
exponential energy to power cities' needs;
the deep Pacific Sea bringing peace to meet man-
kind's plea. [141]

---

[141] *60 Minutes*, CBS TV, November 17, 2019.

In Defense of the Mind

In warfare, intelligence gathering can result in enemy
lives to take,
our military and civilian ones to save. Yet, today's
intolerance
pulls the blinds and hides inside itself. Let's hear what
the opposition has to say
about our way. Can't we grasp the truth, though not
the attitude?
Can we take constructive criticism, discarding the
condemnation?
Yes, we must be wise to enemy deception, not allowing
an apparent gift of peace,
the Trojan horse's men to release.
On that December 7, 1941 terror-struck day,
Japanese diplomats in DC, appearing to allay ten-
sions, in peace,
presented a deception, while Nippon bombers were
destroying our fleet.
What average man or woman in the US
on 9/11, 2001, knew how much Pakistani terrorists,
from childhood indoctrination hated us?
Like Jesus said: "Be wise as a serpent and harmless
as doves."[142]
To have His view of mankind,
we need to understand the enemy's thinking, but not let
it dominate our mind.
Casting down thoughts that destroy who we are, and
not become like the other;
we can forgive, by God's grace, humanity's brother.

[142] From Matthew 10:16

Let us fight in defense of our God-given nation when necessary.

Decide to forgive, as the example of the man, driving the Toyota

with the bumper sticker that read, Pearl Harbor Survivor.[143]

And as much as we can, let's live at peace,

do good, and give the "good news" to our fellowman.

---

[143] Sermon Illustrations, sermoncentral.com

Equitable Patience?

How long should we tempt His sway, His warnings,
not to delay?
How many persuasions for salvation invitations are we
free to refuse,
thinking we have later to choose?
What if another had accepted His call at an early age?
How equitable is it, if patience should have its just day?
Should Christ be made to wait? Did He not become
sin for us,
His death point the way; the cross to demonstrate a love
so worthy?
How many caution lights need be made 'til we yield
to the red,
our aggressive insistence to stop? Run this intersection
at your own risk.
Or, soberly choose to turn from adding sins to the tree,
giving up your life—true liberty.
He sees from beginning to end, even now each
heart of man.
Does He see each rejected attempt a loss,
for each investment in man to count the cost?
Isn't He capable of feeling disappointments and a
broken heart?
From heaven's glory does He, Himself, visit the cross?
Looking at different ages of those He saves; in each case,
isn't it His call to make? Yet, each pursued should keep
this in mind:

to escape the wrath Jesus bore, cover your sins no more,
confess and forsake them to receive
His merciful forgiveness and salvation. [144]

---

[144] Proverbs 28:13 (paraphrased by author)

"A" Game

Like the Lauren Daigle song, "First," what we do should be preceded
by putting God first. Even athletes don't compete 'til
with their coach, they did meet.
How can I train well, without receiving my "A" game?
He is respected as number one, first in capturing the
enemy in his own game, [145]
secondly, providing his own team with performance-enhancing plays.
When interacting with us, is it at His highest power?
Or is it, to learn through Him, lessening our defeats?
Can we be hopeful "winners" by consistently
losing by less,
Him challenging us for our best? To become in this
world like His Son,
we can find that second wind, relying on His strength in
our weakness
to begin. He remembers that of dust we were made.
In His regimen, in maturity's time, we'll find
our upgrade.
He's never less than, the Great I Am, yet like a good Dad,
lifts us over each curb, holding our hand and speaking
an encouraging Word.
I've experienced my own mismanaged time, when in
haste, I'd leave my place.
To gain each day's victory, He'll provide the strategy.
Like a quarterback dependent on Him, this Coach will
make the calls.
I can hear only if I've put on salvation's helmet.

---

[145] I Corinthians 3:13b

Am I loving the body I'm in—taking proper care, giving
it early morning energy,
a good breakfast inside? After all, in me, He abides.
Prepare for midday energy's lack, a healthy lunch or
nutritional snack.
Have I dressed for the part to sell myself for the all-in
role today
in this well-scripted play?
All who've experienced His grasp, know His strength.
You can't outwrestle Him. Yet, we know to find
our strength;
like in judo, we must use His push and pull.
Most important, He has instilled His life within.
He's a Spirit you know, so, through us, for His
Spirit to flow,
we should pray, "Fill me afresh today!"

Change

What if the caterpillar stayed the same? What if he
refused to change;
set in his ways? If he could see his final purpose,
would the fright of groundless height rob him of
winged-flight?
Without the ability to reason to flutter or fly, its origi-
nator placed instinct inside.
What if a peach were only a pit, never a succulent
treat to eat;
only less than its best, just *pityful?* We see adaptation
in nature's
creation, within a species, if not to thrive, at least
to survive.
In the planner's mind, we find genetics design. Though
for the Maker's plan to unfold
steadfast throughout each year, change must occur.
For God's image to be expressed as human, there had to
be a him and a her.
In bonding matrimony, only change in both can
bring harmony.
Then again, each living thing needs offspring, for each
kind to leave an ancestral line.
What if mankind refused to have sex, where would
you be? To
increase the attraction, prompting action, this planner
before reasoning would begin placed instinct within.
Before any retractions can arise; chemical triggers, hor-
monal changes,
euphoric emotions—all bring forth the pleasur-
able action.

Fertile seed and egg combine, yielding progeny after
its own kind.
One who goes from single living to parenting would
probably admit,
I could have been more prepared for this.
Yet, "God puts the solitary in families."[146] Perhaps, our
Spirit-Teacher
would have helped us more if we were willing to change.
If changes lead us to progress; conversely, does our
insistent resistance
lead to growth's regress? Life's changes can be hard, but
to surrender
to the Savior's plan, I'll find trust and peace in the
Great I AM.

---

[146] Psalm 68:6

Freeing

Faith isn't the absence of fear,
like a life preserver in water isn't the absence of water.
Just take hold and hold on for all you've got.
It was tossed to you by the Lifeguard who rescues.
And, when you've held on strong, His boat of safety will
come along.
Stand upon the Rock, though far from the comforting
wooden dock.
A paradox it seems, that the invisible is evidence of the
irrefutable.
Though a natural father yells, "Jump!
And the child is caught in laughter and delight,
what can this supernatural Being do when you know
He's always there for you?
Choose faith in Him to follow, forsaking
self-preservation,
to fulfill His good plans, preemptive, bringing
transformation.

Pick Me

Filling out a hopeful entry, a contestant I would be.
Perhaps you could fill in a fitting analogy?
Was I smart enough? Liked enough? What they're
looking for?
Would the performance I did favor a quid pro quo?
My id cries, "Pick me, pick me, pick me!
Why can't I refrain from what all these thoughts entail?
I'm like a train speeding along this monorail.
Subconsciously, I choose a distraction. To my detriment,
I should have chosen a healthier infraction. Deliver me
from sweet food addictions, abandoning my convictions!
Binge-watching movies on TV! I know the answer!
Before acceptance or rejection, I relieve perfection.
God's love makes me free! I decide for myself. Happily,
I pick me.

Chapter 7

Family Plan

Family Plan [147]

I believe God has a plan for each family's clan.
He's the Father of each dysfunctional family, as well as
those living in harmony.
Jacob, throughout his life had children from each wife,
four to count,
who bore unto him, twelve sons and one daughter.
Seven came forth from Leah, Rachel's weak-eyed sister.
For a long while,
Rachel's womb resembled an empty tomb. Eventually
she did conceive two—
Joseph and Benjamin—though in bearing the last for
Jacob, her guy, she would die.
Also, Jacob's other two wives, Zilpah and Bilhah,
bore two apiece, to make the family complete.
The favor Jacob showed toward Joseph would lead to
jealousy and envy—
the many-colored extravagant coat, in his brothers' eyes,
made Joseph a constant irritancy and a glaring specialty.
Cornered on the desert prairie,
beaten by these irate brothers, then held to be sold
into slavery,
little did they know that one day, he would be
the key to God's family plan for reconciliation.
To make a long story short, I invite you to read the
Joseph story. [148]
Within the patriarch's clan, a man named Judah
would be the ancestor of Yeshua, Messiah,
to save the households of man.

---

[147] Genesis 37:15–36, 39–50

[148] Genesis 38

Arranged Marriage [149]

Was it a godly desire that day, when Abraham spoke to
his faithful servant?
He sought to acquire from his home country a wife for
son Isaac.
It was really a long journey from this land God had
promised him,
back to where he was from, Ur of the Chaldeans. He
might have thought
by now, Sarah would have wanted to see, like me, for
Isaac a bride to be.
By an oath, he made this trusted servant agree to this
matchmaking plan
before his journey would begin, saying,
the God whom he served will go before him.
The servant needed help with this treasured caravan.
He brought men to help with the ten camels, laden
with goods.
The servant upon reaching the town, found, a well-stop.
Perhaps he did think, *even virgin girls need a drink.* This
man, to solve this mystery, knew
only God could provide the proper bride to be by
Isaac's side.
The servant did pray, *God, send a virgin girl, to whom I
will say, "Please give me a little water from your jug." And
she shall reply, Yes, have a drink, and I will water your
camels too.*
In truth, a heart of hospitality did Rebekah show,
answering back almost exactly, to Isaac's proxy.
It was quite a workout, extremely generous
that did ensue

---

to quench ten thirsty camels too.

For her, in strength to rely,
I suspect there was a large water trough nearby.

Favor from this stranger toward her yielded gold jewelry.

He inquired, who's your father? Would he have room for them to stay the night?

Just a thought here, Isaac was born to his parents' beyond-
childbearing years. To make him and Rebekah age
compatible,
God would skip a generation, making Abraham's brother
Nahor, her father Bethuel's father, yes her grandfather.

So, upon Rebekah's return, Laban her brother would check out this man

as a protective brother should. Trusting in what his sister had said, in kind, he invited

these servants to his home to dine, and he cared for the camels too.

The chosen servant of Abraham did confide, what his master did decide,

a Canaanite wife wouldn't compare to the women who came from back here.

The servant would convey what Abraham did say,
"An angel will go with you and will make your mission successful."

He spoke of how God in his love and faithfulness, had with wealth, this trusting
Abraham, blessed.

He revealed the words at the well he did pray. And how, even before he could voice them today, came Rebekah in beauty's array.

Seriously, it was no joke, this sign from her, saying the words she would speak.

Then Laban and her dad agreed that this must be God's
plan; to let Isaac take Rebekah's hand.
When asked to stay ten more days, the servant did relay,
I must not delay.
Even on short notice Rebekah replied, "Yes, I will go."
When they arrived,
from a distance the servant identified Isaac to Rebekah
in modesty with veil,
her face she did hide, ready to take her place at his side.
This arranged marriage would find the love of
Isaac's life.
Another great woman would bring comfort and
love's company
at the loss of his mother. With this lesson, if you're
looking for a mate,
ask the Lord, 'If it's to be, pick the one specifically and
bring that one to me.'

Relative Space

When I watch HGTV, I love to see, mostly,
how the open floor concept provides all to embrace
greater living space.
To take out some walls, giving sight to what's happening
does combine
a view of family and guests in mind.
When looking for a new house, many couples seek a
comfortable bedroom
with bathroom attached for parental visits,
or to accompany or care for an aging father or mother.
What if modern home designs, giving space and
convenience,
existed in Jesus's time? Perhaps comfort would have
challenged
the cultural norm that took less space to get along.
Then again,
on the whole, it could have led to greater
activity to flow.
But constructing homes in Jesus's day led to
closer quarters
for abiding sons and daughters living together.
We see an example when Jesus went to the home of
Andrew and Simon.
Simon's wife's mother lay there, whom Jesus healed of
a fever. [150]
Arranged marriages led to a groom, building onto his
dad's house, an extra room.
As a patriarchy, the father's decision released the provi-
sion. He would decide

---

[150]   Mark 1:29–30

and tell his son: now your addition's done. Go get your
bride.[151] Then children,
children trained up in the way they should go, awaited
a king to bring a kingdom less
hostile than the Roman one.[152] Generational blessings
would come from
sons, daughters, aunts, uncles, nephews, cousins;
less space in close proximity, seeking godly harmony. [153]

---

[151] Proverbs 22:6

[152] *Marriage and Family at the Time of Jesus,* March 26, 2017, Msgr.
Charles Pope

[153] Ibid.

Family Intervention [154]

Things were getting too crazy. They were concerned for
His safety.
The crowd was demanding; the push and shove
nearly crushing.
Outside the door, a mother concerned for her son, had
come along with His brethren.
In apprehension, this family sought Him for an
intervention.
Would her boy's passion for ministry outdo His mind's
emotional capacity?
They heard the screams of demons leaving, the fren-
zied sounds of
people seeking healings for to touch the iconic one,
a prophet of God who the people thought
belonged to them.
The mob ignored His kin's affection.
This family might have wondered:
would his disciples ensure His protection?
Crowded out, all the family could do that day was to get
word to Him.
The message was passed through: "Your family outside
is asking for you."
Desiring to lead them, too, with all the fol-
lowers that day,
Jesus would say: His mother and His brothers are they
who hear the word of God, and obey.

---

[154] Luke 8:19–21

Effort's Win

Sometimes you can see a businessman or
businesswoman
in a conference meeting, called out due to a
daughter or a son,
for a family need. Many movies or TV themes reflect this
reality: the career employee
who gave less than a backseat to their family.
Perhaps insecurity, not money, set for them that priority.
Then again, different interests of the male and the
female of our species
has led him or her down the path of least resistance.
As Professor Henry Higgins would ponder, with chin
in his hand,
"Why can't a woman be more like a man?" [155]
A mother with her children would wonder,
why can't my work-prone husband
spend with us, more family time together?
Let's set the scene. Let's stage an intervention, much like
the family
of an alcoholic for their loved one's comprehension.
Invite truth in.
Overwhelm denial with multiple examples. Though a
feeling of disgrace
likely will take place, let's hold the mirror to their face.
Let honesty appear, confronting the grip of fear in unity,
love's concern for one held dear. By joining action
to prayer,

---

[155] From the movie, *My Fair Lady*, Rex Harrison sings. Composers Alan Jay Lerner and Frederick Lowe.

together, we invoke God's power to catch and release chronic defeat.

Rejoice! He's not through with you. Working with Him together,

He'll take on the whole family too. A common goal to please Him brings unity.

Like tumblers falling into place, His grace opens the locks upon our hearts,

His presence to flow. Spirit's healing, like efforts twin, anoints to release freedom's win.

Chapter 8

A Dream, Vision, Visual Arts, Music, and Dance

Same Page [156]

I felt a strong desire to meet with the author.
The book had captured my affection. To hear Him
read from it
would lift my spirit and gain insight, hearing His tone,
like your best friend's voice over the phone.
On the Q & A, could His definitive voice bring
clarity to the parts that puzzled me?
Had I captured the spirit of His heart, this ancient sage?
Had we been on the same page?

I had an invitation from Him. Arriving, my sur-
prise showed
both without and within. Other followers, He had
invited to this homey den.
The poster over His head read: my book is of no private
interpretation.
Reading His work, I felt personally,
He was diagnosing, analyzing, and ordering a prescrip-
tion for me.
But, looking around the room, I did see,
faces aglow with a unified love that
matched the words on the banner above:
This book is of no private interpretation.

---

[156] This is from a dream I had

Befriended (about a man I pictured in my head)

He was conversing in his mind with his only three:
lonely by choice, this guy. His company: me,
myself, and I.
To me, a challenge right before my eyes; someone I
viewed redeemable.
Yet distrust and fear, like a wild creature, peered
out from his eyes. So, if I in some way could
befriend him,
I'd consider him a trophy prize. To close the distance
and relate,
I'd need the right words to say. Maybe body language
and another smile to broach,
to convey a non-threatening verbal approach.
I ventured out with a nod and a grin, showing
acceptance.
In response; his smile, like a short bungie cord, snapped
back quickly,
too swift to enjoy the stretching expanse.
Smiling again, I came closer, nodding to the double DD
doors across the street.
You look cold, my friend, "Would you have a hot drink
and a donut with me;
my treat?" I could see his fleeing thought, then he
defaulted to
the rut in his mind.
"No, thanks anyway, I'm fine.

Turning his shoulder squarely
to face the comforting coffee shop across the street,
placing four ones in his hand, smiling freely,
I spoke the words so true
that had harpooned my formerly hard heart,
"Jesus loves you."

Picture Puzzle

It was a simple child's puzzle. But it held a mystery.
The picture on the front of the box displayed the world,
with continents in entirety:
a few land colors, with deep-blue seas.
Large pieces to please, for a child of five or four,
solvable on a table or floor.
Once complete, it showed a picture of the world.
And what was the mystery for a child to find?
Flipping it over easily with thin pieces that tightly fit,
revealed the image of a contemplative face:
the one who made it;
Jesus, Maker of the whole world,
longing to make the surrendered pieces of our
lives whole.

Impressionism—the Big Plan

I loved the work but didn't know why.
Smears of thick paint on a large canvas,
blurry figures, no sense.
The artist noticed my stare
and, leaving his comfortable, observable chair,
grabbed my hand, accompanying me
to an open-room doorway rather quickly.
He turned me around toward the painting.
Look now, my man. Do you see my plan?
It was me, standing too close to see.
Now it was as clear as can be.
A lively street scene peered at me.
A marketplace of shoppers standing by fruit stands,
randomly clutching grocery bags in hands.
I said, maybe the world makes
more sense the further the view you take.
Then I can know the artist's plan,
especially when He takes my hand.

Jazz Group

Like a tight team, did that jazz group stream.
The sax skippin' up the scale. I'm feeling the notes
in between,
can't help tappin' my feet, percussion's beat
capturing me.
The bass and the drums diggin' each's contributions.
Now a pause opens for the piano's interpretation,
with rifts to lift, though returning, making the tempo fit.
There's so much respect, takin' turns, bowing to anoth-
er's soul yearns.
This musical train, all designed to ride the guiderail,
fast, slow, together. Could it get any better?
What's that bass have to say? We lean in to hear the gut-
felt vibration.
The sax comes back, blaring in, then the piano foremost,
winding the group down, so hip.
What a ride, this round-trip!

Fun Spark

Channel surfing one Sunday afternoon, I entered a view so plain,
so straight. I had to "Czech" the program out. It was polka dancing!
Round and round, as accordion and saxophones did sound,
blended harmonies did provide, couple-unions side-by-side,
amazingly, not to collide. Polka fans poured out like hockey players to the ice.
The thought occurred, *when we're both retired, could this be, for my wife and me?*
Colorful Midwest gals wearing white, with red-trimmed skirts, men in bright
shirts, moved with automatic ease, like trainees to perform; an audience of
viewers they did please. The only acceptable "Pole"-dancing to me,
each complete by their cheek-to-cheek.
Age made no difference, moving in pairs, seemingly oblivious to others near,
all grabbing partners: daughters with mothers, big sisters with little brothers;
for music and rhythm were in the air.
Again, *would my wife think it so square, to forget her rock-and-roll past to become a polka pair?*
These happy times we could share, when work wanes and retirement living
turns, full swing.

Chapter 9

Humor and Nonsense

Fun Time

In the navy, transient sailors in barracks await authorizations
to their next duty stations. When I was one, daily jobs were dealt out
to keep us from lingering about. One day a sailor and I were soon
assigned to clean a large bathroom, and a walk-in nearby showering place.
The adjoined shower room had curb-like partitions to step over, keeping the
waters flow only in the showering area to go.
My co-worker and I were opposites in size. And I surmised,
more of an extrovert was he, more introvert—me. He was close to six feet tall,
I, not nearly as close, perhaps five-five at most. He was somewhat overweight,
with a Buddha belly to crate. Thin was my appeal, if you like the shape of an eel. We would get all wet. We were told:
"It's best to work without clothes."
He had a plan in mind, but first a digression he'd find.
He turned the water on, full blast, hot, the walls to rinse down.
To the floor, the water did go, several inches or so accu-mulating before it drained.
When he soaped himself up, I thought he was mixing work with hygiene,
himself to clean. Yet, he got belly down in that huge stall,

using his arms, like flippers, penguin-like he scooted
from wall-to-wall.
The laughter was contagious. Seemingly, almost insane,
I soaped up, doing the same.
His smile and style mimicked a bottlenose dol-
phin, and me,
more like a seal. Squeals of joy with glee,
echoed off walls as we competed for glide and speed.
Eventually we completed our assigned duty.
Fortunately, no one in authority was there to see.
It was such a joyful break
from the boredom, as we did our orders await.

Abrupt Disgust

This poem carries a warning: recommended not to be
read while you eat or drink.
On my inside job one day, outside city workers hit the
water main
to our building. We took an early work break,
for water was a necessary ingredient for the
product we made.
We enjoyed social talk while still on the clock. As we
were sipping
our coffee, someone remembered previously the pot had
been empty.
The question arose: so, how was the new coffee brewed
without any H_2O?
Robert, who usually drank at least five cups a day, had
found a way.
Enjoying the new brew, we still didn't have a clue.
Feeling thankful, gave way to Robert's resolve,
the mystery was solved—yet to him no one
would thank;
for he had filled the pot full with water from a
toilet tank.
Perhaps, considered the leading pastor in our city, new-
comers to his church,
he loved conversations on home visitations. [157]
He'd chat and sit, acquainting himself with by his warm
and friendly smile,
getting to know each person after a while.

---

[157] Pastor Homer G. Lindsay Jr. (July 10, 1927—February 14, 2000,
First Baptist Church, Jacksonville, Florida

On one of these home calls he was welcomed by a
friendly elderly lady.
People did see, from his rather large size, that he did
like to eat.
Wrapping up his time taken, he looked down to
see missing,
all the peanuts in the dish he had eaten. Offering
an apology:
I'm so sorry for my manners, I ate all the peanuts on
the table.
She dismissingly, lightly scoffed, that's quite OK,
with my bad teeth, all I can do is gum the chocolate off.

African Man

I have a humorous and endearing story to share.
I attended a fundraiser luncheon for an organization
whose name spoke their belief: World Relief.
Africans, Asians, South, Central, and North Americans
were there;
United in the persuasion that refugees to our land
each could use a helping hand.
Women, dressed in their native attire, served foods—
family-made recipes that generational
years did acquire. Smiling faces greeted everyone.
Friends received customary
greetings expressed in body language, and in their
familiar foreign tongues.
>After coffee, tea, a light meal, and a sweet treat,
>like baklava, we settled down,
>with anticipation of an informative presentation.
>Gratitude was expressed in
>behalf of those whose food did us bless. The host
>gave credit to those whose time
>and hospitable talents made this event possible.
>A man from Sudan who presently works for this
>nonprofit organization was
>introduced to the clapping of hands.
>Though now such an asset to this charitable
>profit, he told of his story of settlement in
>this new land.
>Many bright men and women would have to start
>all over again,
>at the bottom of the economic ladder, as
>low wage earners to make a living. With tenacity,

English language classes, in
afterwork hours, would lead to greater wage capacity,
climbing rungs on that promotion ladder.
On his first job at the processing plant, American
workers would greet
him with "What's up? Puzzled he would look up,
then around, but nothing unordinary would be
found. He and another refugee
from his homeland would ride the bus to
work each day.
Saving, in time they would share a car. Of
course, a new
challenge faced the two. The bus driver knew the way.
Now, how do we get to work each day?
They decided they'd follow the bus.
I'm thinking, it must have
been before GPS. The bus driver felt unease,
for every stop and go he would
make, they also did take. He told the police.
An officer pulled them over. Upon
hearing their reasoning,
he laughed heartily and said, "Follow me."
Their simple explanation brought a generous act:
he guided them to their current vocation.
Speaking at the event, this man did evoke
sympathy for refugees as he spoke.
We laughed and sighed. Some would give donations.
Newcomers bonded with citizens who wel-
comed as one,
all to our homeland, who had come.

Rhyme, for or Not for Reason

Maybe it's an id thing with me. When I hear a phrase or
a sentence with rhyming words, my soul almost leaps
from my body!
I find myself near ecstasy, when advertisers make
appeals using poetry.
I liked the slogan for a caring chimney-cleaning service—
"We get the flue for You."
Then there's the bigger market reached by pro-
moting soccer
using poetry, to the physical play of Lionel Messi.
To the narration of the "If" poem by Rudyard Kipling,
with rhyme and rhythm combined—exciting.
By hearing victims speaking out on a "beat bullying"
poem on YouTube,
we see this abuse despicable and no longer acceptable.
When I see the potential loss in decisions, that, with a
little more time,
could have been made with rhyme in mind,
it triggers in me the unkind. It's like the ape in the fic-
tional story,
who, at the sound of the bell, will kill violently,
then stuff the body up the chimney. [158]
OK, so my example is a hyperbole. I'm not unkind to
that degree.
For another example, I heard on the Tuesday
morning news:
The Presidential Debate would be on TV that eve. And
they called this debate, "The

---

[158] "The Murders in the Rue Morgue," Edgar Allen Poe, 1831

Showdown in Cleveland." My rage engaged! No! cried
out my soul!
The promoters should have chosen Detroit.
The invitational phrase could have been:
"The Showdown in Motown!"

I Caught a Poem Today

I caught a poem today. It lifted and made me sway;
thus, sprang a lively step, a confidence met.
Complaining voices roll off me like raindrops on a
polished car.
Happy thoughts come during traffic stops.
What can this be, this unforeseen joy rising up in me?
I'll sidestep all conflict, treat others, one and all
with respect,
negotiate a perceived reject with a disarming smile. All
the while,
I'll protect this rare mood I'm in. I'll do my best to
impress it upon my mind,
capturing this state by prolonging it with an appro-
priate song.
If challenged to defend my actions,
I will state my case as a lawyer with a well-
equipped defense.
Should I perceive a hung jury without consensus,
I'll tip the persuasion by presenting plaintiff evidence.
In any way, logically or illogically, it will be the
right way,
for I caught a poem today.

Overflow

There once was a man named Michael McTardy,
though chronically late for work,
his excuses evoked laughter so hearty.
Every quip came with great wit
and left pictures in our minds that,
throughout the day, would not go away.
These memories, bubbling with joy, did overflow,
filling our souls,
and kept us near and dear. We all laughed with
achy frames,
knowing he was too good to get fired,
when he called to say "I'll be in late, I'm tired."
Alas, unexpectedly, Michael did pass.
His co-workers sadly attended his funeral.
At the graveside burial,
a spirit of mirth was birthed,
as the mourners read the words
on McTardy's grave:
Johnson & Johnson,
Please don't throw
my time card away;
I'll be back for last week's pay.

Chapter 10

Two Present Age Parables

A Frightful Encounter [159]

I heard a story, whether true or not; it illustrates a per-
ceived, suspenseful plot.

So, it goes: years ago, before CB radios, or any such,
communication

in trucks, a truckdriver tailed a woman driving her car.
From his cab so high, he could look down and see
with his eyes,

a man crouched behind the woman's driver seat. The
woman driving on a well-traveled

highway, noticed that day, being closely followed by a
truckdriver. She turned off to a

main road. Behind her, he did also. Then when she sped
up, so did he.

Noticing a serious look on his face, at the next intersec-
tion's light she did stop,

making a sharp right she quickened the pace.

Next, at the first light, she made a left and sped away,
hoping to put herself out of sight. Still in her rearview
mirror, this truck would closely

appear. Shaking with fear, adrenaline flowing, an idea
came to her.

She saw a dirt side road, and in the distance, a conve-
nience store. Speeding up she

floored it, turning, then stopping her car by the pumps.
She flew out the driver's door, running toward the store.
Instantly, the driver bolted too. He quickly
opened the door

behind her driver-seat. Holding the man secure before
he could flee,

---

[159] *Deseret.com, Tale of Backseat Killer is Similar to News Stories*

this rescuer loudly called out to her: Have the store call the police!

You may ask, what's the point? It's an analogy meant to show clear,

if God were the pursuer and the woman in danger, the wrong one she did fear. Misunderstanding this one so good,

He only wanted to save her from harmful attack.

The selfish, destructive one He did hold away, keeping her safe that suspenseful day.

Like this person, fearing the good one trailing, believing a lie; God wants no harm, but

the best for you. Fear not; He's not the one behind you to do harm, but to trust Him each

day, He'll lead you to travel with Him into Eternal Life's Way!

Field Birds and a Boy

I heard a story told me by a friend of sinners, who tells
it on the streets.
It's an old story. I've read some versions online, but I like
my friend's just fine.
It gives a mental picture and leaves a decision with
the hearer.
As you picture it through, ask yourself who you relate to.
The story goes back a way. So, here it is:
A man was on the street one day. A dirty-faced, unkempt
boy walked his way.
The boy, around ten, was with one hand, swinging an
old, battered bird cage.
In the other, the man observed a stout stick. There were
birds in the bottom of the cage,
shivering and looking sick. "Son, what's in the cage?
"The boy, acting arrogant for his
age, replied, "Some wild birds I caught early today.
They're for my play."
"So, what will you do with them when you're done?"
Upon this,
the boy across the metal bars raked his stick.
Then, like a fencer, forward, he thrusted it. "I'm going to
have fun, ruffle them
up, and pull some feathers out. After that, I'll feed them
to my cat.
"Can I buy them from you?" "They are field birds; got
no value,"
the boy answered him. Again, the man enquired, "How
much you want for them?"

Raising his hand to his chin, reluctantly with a disap-
pointed expression, "I'll take a ten."
Into the boy's hand, the man placed two fives. The boy
left in his pride.
When reaching home, outside, the man set the
cage down.
Scarcely making a sound, he gently coaxed the birds
to come out.
They just shivered and did shake, choosing the cage not
to vacate.
Isn't this an analogy to what Jesus has done, set-
ting us free?
For, He asked, concerning birds: "Are you not of more
value than they?" [160]
He paid the price to set the captives free! Don't believe
the devil's lie.
Fly, free birds! Fly free!

Jim -With this book of poems I invite the reader to
relate to me, and evaluate their own thoughts in life's
journey. Hopefully those who have already decided to
follow Jesus will see a variety of poems that show a pro-
gressive discovery of knowing Jesus, and can acquaint
themselves to the goodness of the Lord in their personal
walk with Him.

Marc Swan—a retired vocational rehabilitation coun-
selor and writer, recent poetry collection *all it would
take,* tall lighthouse London UK. In "Looking Up! An
Invitation to Compare Life Experience with Eternal
Truth," James T Edwards blends contemporary thought

---

[160] Mathew 6:26

with Biblical script and universal messages captured in a flowing verse. His poem "Same Difference" speaks to the lineage of racial injustice that haunts all of our lives, and brings the reader to an awareness of what true friendship can mean. Jim incorporates old movies, TV shows, and adages to open the door of understanding, compassion and hope that many seem to have forgotten.

Ken Johns—retired policeman. Thanks Jim, for sharing your heart and memories with the rest of us. As a young boy in junior high I began reading for enjoyment. This developed into a love for reading that has continued throughout my life. Though mostly interested in history, I read little poetry. Then I learned that my friend Jim had written a book with poetry. I read his book and could not put it down! His poems were stories that moved me.

Shari McGriff—Author, Professor and Book Coach, shapingculturethroughstory.com Jim Edwards is a storyteller in poem form. Each poem relays a lesson of love, whether it's Jesus' love for Mary Magdalene in "Extravagant Love Received," or the love of an Iranian visitor for America when he wants to see the Statue of Liberty in "Two displays," or the love Jim has for his wife when he first pursues her in "Liquid Love." You'll enjoy the lyrical stories.

Author Biography -Jim was born and raised in Binghamton, New York. He left to serve in the Navy for four years. After the service, he attended and graduated from Florida State University with a B.S. in Marketing/

Management. He worked for over thirty years in the optical industry in Jacksonville, Florida, where he lives and is retired today. He served as a Prayer Coordinator at the Vineyard Church, as a volunteer with Big Brother, Big Sister, with World Relief, and visited the Gerontology Center with a worship/prayer team for over ten years. He has had the desire to write poetry return to him from a youth for the last four years. He is married to Donna, his wife of thirty-eight years, and has a daughter, Karen.